# ABOUT WORDSWORTH AND WHITEHEAD

# ABOUT WORDSWORTH
# AND WHITEHEAD

## *A Prelude to Philosophy*

## by

## Alexander P. Cappon

Philosophical Library

New York

Cappon, Alexander Patterson, 1900-
    About Wordsworth and Whitehead.

    Includes bibliographical references.
    1. Whitehead, Alfred North, 1861-1947.
    2. Wordsworth, William, 1770-1850 — Influence —
Whitehead. I. Title.
B1674.W354C36          192    81-80937
ISBN 0-8022-2386-9              AACR2

Overseas distributor: George Prior Ltd.
52-54 High Holborn, London WC1V 6RL, England

To my beloved wife

Dorothy Churchill Cappon

who has read thoughtfully

every sentence of this book

more than once, sharing with me her reflections

upon them

## Contents

## Acknowledgments

In the volume *About Wordsworth and Whitehead* there are many acknowledgments that must be made to friends and others — some of whom are not now living. The authors who are under discussion in the successive chapters have themselves of course given a great deal, which will be very evident in the book itself. And Wordsworthian scholars are so many that the only possibility is to suggest a very profound indebtedness to these writers. Two of them especially come to mind for specific note: Ernest De Selincourt, definitive editor of *The Prelude* in its various forms, and Melvin P. Rader. The work of the latter has been philosophically foundational for a great many years.

The help of my wife, Dorothy Churchill Cappon, has been beyond words. The dedication of this volume speaks of this. Nor can I express adequately the help that was given by my daughter, Frances Cappon Geer, and my brother, John A. Cappon. In this book I have found it impossible to avoid the use of the word "we" because of what I owe to these three.

Scholars who have written penetratingly on Whitehead are many and their names could fill pages. Among those who come at once to mind are Victor Lowe, A.H. Johnson, Charles Hartshorne, Craig R. Eisendrath, Harold B. Dunkel, John W. Lango, Paul Arthur Schilpp, and Arthur Murphy. I must further express my appreciation of the kindnesses of Director Dagobert D. Runes and Associate Director Rose Morse and others of Philosophical Library, Publishers. Material quoted from various books will be acknowledged in the footnotes to the chapters that follow, including full statements of the names of the publishers themselves, to whom I wish now also to express my special thanks.

Likewise of great importance to me in my work have been my mother and father, Carl Henry Grabo, Frank K. Kelly, Kenneth Burke, Robert Morss Lovett, William M. Ryan, John Livingston Lowes, George Herbert Mead, Harold Buschman, David Ray, Raymond Bragg, William L. Crain, Theodore Brameld, and Bernard P. Churchill. For the main part I have omitted mention of titles or honors of these persons who have helped me. Herwig Zauchenberger deserves thanks.

Publishers have been of value to me, as they are to all mankind: Cambridge University Press has been an important publisher of Whitehead, as has the Macmillan Company. Oxford University press, publisher of the 1805 *Prelude* written by Wordsworth, has been of vital value and also deserves special acknowledgement.

To librarians and to cities I owe a great deal: Immediate mention should appear with regard to the Widener and Houghton Libraries at Harvard, the libraries at Yale and the University of Chicago, that of Columbia University in New York, as well as libraries in Milwaukee, Tulsa, and the University of Kansas. I would also express gratitude to the Library of Congress, the British Museum, and to the libraries and librarians in Paris, as well as in Seattle — including the library of the University of Washington, where I taught.

Likewise my appreciation goes to the library of Washington University of St. Louis and that of Montana State University. This list and the list of friends and teachers to whom I owe much cannot be complete. The names of Philip Schyler Allen, President James C. Olson of the University of Missouri, Vivian Mowry, Deborah D. Feingold, Dorothy Sohm Metz, Robert Willson, Robert Farnsworth, James Weber Linn, and my sister Charlotte Beatrice Blackmun should be added, by no means as an afterthought, with my very warm appreciation.

The help of librarians in the Kansas City Public Library has been extended to me again and again, far beyond any line of duty, to my everlasting gratitude, and likewise the help of the University of Missouri at Kansas City in itself and Chancellor George A. Russell must receive grateful mention, along with the University librarian, Kenneth J. LaBudde.

Alexander P. Cappon
University of Missouri —
Kansas City

## Introduction: The Problem

Can it be said that there is a kinship of thought between William Wordsworth and Alfred North Whitehead? Is Wordsworth a great enough figure for such kinship really to exist? The reader might doubt that an intellectual affinity — any important intellectual affinity between them — could exist, in view of the stature of Whitehead, who has been in some circles mentioned as the greatest philosopher of the twentieth century. Thoughtful people at times have felt mysteriously attracted to Whitehead's writings, but parts of his works have often been held to be very difficult. One is inclined to seek some sort of key to the difficulties. But where is such a key to be found? The work of Wordsworth, surprisingly enough, provides something of a key to Whitehead. The thinking of Wordsworth in his poem *The Prelude*, as we shall see, opens a door to many reflections, among which are the relationships of the poet's thought to a world-view such as Whitehead's. Is it possible that the poet and the philosopher, as seen together, can be made to appear in a new, late twentieth-century light? Could recent reflection be of value in a reading of them?

In approaching Wordsworth and Whitehead according to our plan we feel it is best at the earlier stages to avoid certain philosophical technicalities, many of which are unnecessary to our purpose, and to move somewhat gradually toward the profounder substance of Whitehead's thought. This gradual approach is helped through reflecting on the relationship of his

1

ideas to the life and experience of Wordsworth. The poet's life itself is a part of this book. Brief observations concerning philosophy along with facts about Wordsworth's life can thus be introduced from time to time as the problems of the modern world are intermittently considered. References to Whitehead's conceptions will, however, be increasingly stressed, and at later stages it may seem that the work being presented is more involved in Whitehead than in the poet. The scope of Whitehead's philosophy is wide and it requires increased attention, especially in its later developments.

But Wordsworth's thought itself seems also to have grown in complexity, especially as he proceeded in his writing of *The Prelude*. The final material of the poem moves toward subtleties that are exceedingly challenging to the person who is seeking to understand him fully. His thought is expansive, and the same is true of the thinking of Whitehead although in a different sense. The later material of *The Prelude* may be more clearly followed by seeing it in relation to the thought of Whitehead. At times it might almost seem that Whitehead was greatly influenced by a reading of *The Prelude* itself, and that this influence grew as he went on in his thinking. But this need not be asserted, although without doubt he did appreciate Wordsworth greatly as we shall see.

A conception of the meaning of philosophy itself emerges in considering the thought of Whitehead and Wordsworth. Philosophy, as viewed by Whitehead, requires a patient seeking of love and wisdom, and a penetration far beyond the surface of things. There is a love that may result from the quest of wisdom itself. Some reference to twentieth-century philosophy other than that of Whitehead will be of interest in relation to Wordsworth, but the main purpose in this book is to center on Whitehead and his thought of importance to the most creative currents of the twentieth century. Biographical material will appear now and then, although, as we have previously suggested, it is secondary.

From the time that a possible kinship of Whitehead and Wordsworth presented itself for reflection, the relationship has been seen to be more complex than it at first appeared to be. Whitehead as a philosopher is closer to Wordsworth, we have come to believe, than any other philosopher of the twentieth century. Nevertheless, it might be asked, are they still not very far apart? An answer to this question will develop in what follows. There is a broader problem, also, about which the reader may wonder. Are we not today, it may be asked, distant as the poles from authors such as Wordsworth? Can we, with our social views, even think of ourselves in relation to such strangers? One possible answer is that perhaps we are far closer than we realize to Wordsworth and even to the countless figures of a more remote past. Are we not, after all — including the people of the past and present — one human family, as Whitehead indeed believes? That is a question to take into account in what follows. Perhaps in addition we need to be much closer than we are to all the human beings of our own time. Such closeness is difficult to attain; it requires reflection upon the past and the present, along with the pondering of the problems of harmony and disharmony, leading ultimately to a conscious need of peace, a matter so involved that one almost despairs. One wonders whether inner peace in any sense can ever be attained. Whitehead wrote, as a climax, an entire chapter on "Peace" in *Adventures of Ideas*. We, naturally, have been influenced by the subject.

This book will, accordingly, be concerned to some extent with peace — including the peace of the self — along with the question of democracy in the twentieth century, a democracy of both action and the spirit. Such matters are important in the thinking of Wordsworth and Whitehead. It will be necessary for us to attain a greater measure of inward peace (and of philosophy) before we can, together with others, reach some degree of advance in the outward harmony of nations. But the situation need never be regarded as hopeless. We can in general

3

gain in understanding day by day: that is the very nature of human beings considered singly and as a people. The question of the relationship between Wordsworth and Whitehead will in any case give rise to certain reflections concerning the possibility of an advancing democracy. America tends to think of democracy as a matter of bald declarativeness: we make a declaration or present a manifesto. In such an approach the subject itself is treated in a didactic manner. Propositions are asserted concerning happiness and a person's right to the enjoyment of this emotion.

Viewed somewhat differently, democracy is a speculative concept presenting a gigantic question mark. The same may be said of the concept of peace. We cry aloud for peace, with its benefits and its very necessity, and yet we wonder whether it can ever be, or whether there is even any meaning in the term. We are contradictory. Aside from the two approaches — the declarative, which is a kind of indoctrinating or teaching mode of attack, and the questioning method, which is speculative and exploratory — there are other valuable ways of dealing with these two subjects. One other way would be to consider democracy and peace not externally, as outward, objective things, but internally as they become part of the private structure of the self. We need not suggest that they should be made altogether internal, but the internal should be considered. This internalization is not complete subjectiveness or lawlessness. Implicit here is a problem in philosophic thinking. The world is very wide and the self seems very small, but the two are closely interwoven, as seen in the thought of Wordsworth and Whitehead.

Without attempting to define the concepts of democracy and peace or, indeed, the concept of the self (we can assume a sufficient working notion of them at this point), we will say that they represent a part of the problem of this book. But we can well emphasize the fact that questions about democracy and peace in the world, especially as related to the self, are among the most important which a human being can today strive to understand. Before we can act we must to some extent broadly understand things. The theme to be considered concerns, then, the interrelated, existential thought of a poet of the early nineteenth century and of Whitehead who is a striking figure of the twentieth century.

But why choose Wordsworth rather than another writer of the nineteenth century period? Samuel Coleridge, because of his perceptiveness, could have been the figure here. Like Wordsworth he had a vital reflective interest in democracy. He also had strong concern for philosophy and peace. But Whitehead in a sense chooses Wordsworth for us. In *Science and the Modern World* he presents a discussion of poets he holds are important in expressing tendencies of successive periods, and Wordsworth stands out strikingly among them.

The poets Whitehead selects for his purpose represent a development which he believes has had a significant relation to philosophy. They have a connection, an interweaving, with our feelings and experience. His own thinking at times has been held to be poetical; he stresses in a special way the importance of the emotional and the spiritual, including the philosophical. He selects a number of periods of the past that reveal the way certain developments (which are related to our own time) have occurred. He thinks of Milton's epoch, for example, and its self-certainty, its "untroubled certitude."[1] A special kind of dogmatism was then in the air. After having dealt with Milton's period, he refers, in the next page, to the time of Alexander Pope and to his "jaunty assurance" about the world and its problems. Following this epoch, the poets, as Whitehead points out, become less and less sure of themselves and of their relation to the world. When people are troubled they begin to reflect and ask more profound philosophic questions. This troubled state is a field for philosophic study.

But to come back to Whitehead and his thought about the distressed people in the nineteenth century. There was a

5

tendency in the century preceding our own for those who are thoughtful to become increasingly disturbed and disorganized. They suffered inwardly. This is strikingly true, finally, in the twentieth century. We see it in the novels of our century, for example in Saul Bellow or Thomas Mann. Whitehead's very immediate point of attention on the problem, however, is the nineteenth century where special distresses of mind are notably apparent. And this focus of attention in the philosopher is made clear in certain statements that he makes about the troubled soul, even while his main purpose is to prepare the way for a discussion of science and philosophy and for future hope in relation to the twentieth century.

It might seem that the troubled nineteenth century mood to which we have referred represents a mere truism. The point Whitehead makes in the end, however, is not a simplistic one. Science of course had its bearing on the troubled state of mankind then, and it has now. We all know this. But the ideas Whitehead emphasizes concern certain literary works which he refers to as the "relevant poems"[2] — including Milton's, and works of other writers — for the purpose of his argument. Here psychology and philosophy play a part. These "relevant poems" are relevant not only to the troubled state of a human being's mind, but to the very nature of his perception and intercommunication. In reference to this latter point Whitehead believes that Wordsworth has an important place. The mind itself represents subtle intercommunication.

But more: the poet has a position deserving serious consideration with reference to philosophy generally. Whitehead gives emphasis to the fact that Wordsworth's design for *The Excursion* included exceptional breadth: "A prose preface," Whitehead says (he is referring again to *The Excursion*), "tells us that it is a fragment of a larger projected work, described as 'A philosophical poem containing views of Man, Nature, and Society.'"[3] In this triple reference appearing in the poet's quoted words we have virtually the whole wide scope of

6

philosophy. Two pages later Whitehead refers to "the deepest thinkers" of the poetical movement to which Wordsworth belongs, and he chooses the poet as standing above Coleridge in that development. Wordsworth serves as an illustration of the philosopher's very important observations in the context he then presents.

The purposes that Whitehead has before him as he speaks of Wordsworth do not involve merely the special private wishes of human beings of high social station or the interests of some one person: that is, the interests of individualism. Particularity of this private kind we find exemplified in Alexander Pope's references to his friend Lord Bolingbroke. Pope, as Whitehead ironically implies, addresses attention to the socially-great Lord Bolingbroke, instead of directing attention to God. Whitehead's own philosophic purposes are aimed toward the larger nature of the universe. They concern a "presence" which he feels almost breathes beneath the surface in Wordsworth's works. One example of this, as Whitehead points out, is "the brooding presence of the hills which haunts him." [4] The philosopher himself, we can see, almost becomes a poet as he thinks of Wordsworth here.

What has been said about Whitehead's thinking is only preliminary, and is given here for the purpose of indicating that the term philosophy is a variable, depending upon the philosopher one is considering. To some people the essence of philosophy is analysis. To others it is vision. To still others it is analysis *and* vision, including the aesthetic. Our intent is to look forward toward certain broad philosophic ideas in Whitehead which we believe are important to the future that lies ahead for us, and then to see how these ideas grow to some extent out of a limited past. The limited past we refer to here is the poet Wordsworth himself. Not that the whole scope of Whitehead comes directly from the poet: we would assert no such thing. But the present and the future are illuminated by seeing their relation with a past. And the future is important; it

7

is integrated with the past and present. This is a point that Whitehead himself regularly considers. As he says, we need, among other things, to read history "forwards and backwards." [5] This is the principle which we shall ourselves try to follow. The interest is in the future along with the past.

We have aimed first and foremost, then, to look back from a twentieth-century vantage point, in order to see what Whitehead and Wordsworth, in mutual reinforcement, have to offer us today. We think of Wordsworth as a literary man who is attempting to incorporate into his work some things which have a philosophical tinge. Background to Wordsworth's ideas, we must grant, is important here. But it seemed best not to examine him by going into the remote past. We do not wish to trace the development of his thought down to his own time. To do so would involve ending with early nineteenth-century England. Such a study is an approach that is commonly followed, and it has value. The problem here conceived, however, has been influenced by Whitehead's own philosophy which involves the backward-and-forward movement that has been mentioned. From time to time there will arise again the question: What is the nature of philosophy? The understanding of it is a very large matter in itself. It is elusive. What Whitehead mentions about Wordsworth and the "presence" of the hills is an example of this elusiveness. The mind as communication is another.

Thus far in our introduction we have used quotations from *Science and the Modern World*, perhaps Whitehead's most popular work. But though the volume focuses largely upon science, it is nature, as he points out, that has the main connection with "the presence of the hills," and thus it is nature that the philosopher at the moment is considering in its application to Wordsworth: this and philosophy. Whitehead is preoccupied not only with the presence of the hills but with other things which also seem to haunt Wordsworth. Poetry itself can be haunting.

8

What we have been indicating touches upon the fact that Whitehead's view of the world — his cosmology, as he refers to it — has a relationship to poetry. We have already been concerned with the meaning of philosophy in the reference to the brooding presence of the hills which haunts Wordsworth. There is a factor also in philosophy itself which directly haunts us. This is in part the way in which Whitehead himself thinks of philosophy. Whitehead's world-view is broad; it includes, as we have implied, the aesthetic. In this respect he has an additional affinity with Wordsworth.

Are we all to some extent poets in our needs? We must consider the wide perspective of humanity here. We are not individually completely independent. We are all siblings under the skin. This concept is connected with Whitehead's philosophy. Because of our very incompleteness as human beings, because of our aspiration, and because of our consequent need, there is something that haunts us in the very nature of experience itself. The term philosophy can for our purposes be best understood in relation to existence and experience as treated by such a thinker as Whitehead. A factor which is almost clairvoyant is at times present in his thought. Many readers doubtless have felt this, and it may be one reason why his books have been very widely sold in paperback form, far beyond the sale of John Dewey's volumes — although Dewey's name is now a household word. Interpreters of Whitehead would argue over the point that we are making concerning a possible clairvoyancy in Whitehead. But there is surely something haunting within philosophy itself, according to his own view of it; we find him using this term in its various forms in relation to profound thought. The search made in philosophy — as Whitehead sees it — includes a consideration of three entities which place "before us the problem which," as he says, "haunts the serious thought of mankind." [6]

The triad of entities Whitehead refers to are space, time, and deity. Relationism is a factor here. Whitehead's remark has a connection with the thought of Samuel Alexander, but the important feature of the quoted passage is its connection with Whitehead's independent philosophy. This connection has a bearing on the sense of something divine in our experience on earth. Let us mark particularly his later emphasis upon the sense of what he calls Deity. "The unity of a transcendent universe," he believes, will have its profound effect upon us, along with "the multiplicity of realized actualities" which also have an influence and are therefore important — here by the word "multiplicity," Whitehead would include a perfectly tremendous number of interlaced factors; we paraphrase to some extent his wider thought, but in the sentence from which we have quoted it is made explicit that in his view the unity and the multiplicity will affect us, or "will enter into our experience," through a "sense of Deity." [7] This involves communication and interrelation.

But quite apart from such complexities, and the haunting aura of the term philosophy as Whitehead understands it, there is the fact that the field of philosophy deals with the wide relational views that we may have. In recent decades there have been references to futurism and its relation to extended views. Such extended views guide us in seeing beyond the limited actions connected with the gaining of immediate bread and butter, and meeting other mundane needs such as shelter, important as these are. When we get beyond the everyday plane we tend to seek philosophy: This involves a swiftly-circling view in which some elementary aspects are carried in the back of the mind, or are for the moment out of sight. Here and earlier we have given only a rough or preliminary statement of what must form a part of philosophy. It includes a hurricane of thought.

We have recognized difficulties, as well as values, arising from various interpretations of a largely inclusive world-view, involving "a consciousness which reaches into the future." [8] The needs of a life on earth and the love for one's fellow man (along with peace), we can emphasize again, have also a significant place in Whitehead's thought. His conception of this may be seen even by considering his philosophy of education. He observes that, as one thinks of the balance of the individual and the dire need for an "adaptation of the whole system" of our modern education, our democratic requirements for the community are at present very far from being adequately dealt with. He does not believe that "the needs of a democratic community" can be met simply; the problems are "far from being solved." [9] They cannot be met by specialist education plus mere "general knowledge of a slighter character."

What Whitehead has emphasized is applicable to our problems today. The point that he makes comes down to a need which we have for philosophy of relational structure, broadly considered, but not for a supremely analytical conception of the subject. He favors a philosophy which is close to our existential feelings and our lives. "The make-weight which balances the thoroughness of the specialist intellectual training should be of a radically different kind from purely intellectual analytical knowledge." His position is one that includes aspects of art and the aesthetic, we may say again, and it is here that we would especially bring in poetry as it is connected with Wordsworth's outlook. Wordsworth's poetry should be read attentively while one holds this in mind.

Along with the philosophic aspects of the story that lies ahead, it is to be hoped that a certain amount of help will be given to the reader in his appreciation of some works he had earlier read which we do not even mention. Philosophy, in so far as we can gain knowledge of it, is often an aid to an understanding of both novels and poetry. The search for a philosophy here includes a contemplation of the nature of the expanding social self, along with the involvements of democracy and a sense of inner peace which can come from such expansion. Perhaps all these things comprise what we most deeply mean when at times we speak of democracy as closely integrated with the pursuit of happiness. It is the right to the pursuit itself — as it is concerned with all persons — which is important; here (in socially oriented pursuit) is the focal center to which attention is to be directed. The actual attainment of an expansive happiness enjoyed by the individual in complete indifference to others is not the aim. Such a dubious happiness would have small meaning for the philosopher Whitehead or the poet Wordsworth. Matters pertaining to democracy appear in relation to Wordsworth's experience in the French Revolution. The idea of peace in connection with other topics receives consideration in the latter part of *The Prelude*.

Before us, then, lies the problem of an examination of a poet whose mind — as Whitehead himself implies — has been colored by philosophic considerations. But the survey of Wordsworth will not be directed toward thought about the entire scope of his writings; rather, it will center mainly upon what he has to say in *The Prelude*. In that work he is engaged in self-communication and occupied with his expanding spirit's history. *The Prelude* has been generally regarded as his major work, and we have chosen the 1805 version because it has a closer relation to our time, as well as to Whitehead, than the edition of 1850, which was more conventional, politically and religiously. Had the 1850 *Prelude* been used, questions with regard to democracy and inner peace — not to mention those related more directly to happenings in the outer world — would have received quite different treatment.

The reason that *The Prelude* has been chosen for very special emphasis will bring us back once more to Whitehead. Although he implied a relevance of Wordsworth's poem *The Excursion* to philosophy (as centering upon the individual man, and upon nature, and upon human social relationships), he esteemed *The Prelude* even more highly. In *The Prelude* he finds among other things the element of the profoundly mysterious because of its extraordinary power of grasping "the whole of nature as involved in the tonality of the particular instance." [10] Book One of *The Prelude*, Whitehead holds, is the "greatest poem, by far," that Wordsworth ever wrote.

# Note

Care should be exercised in referring to the precise editions of Whitehead's books which are cited, since various copies of the works have textual differences and disparities in pagination although they might seem to represent identical printings. Likewise, in the use of Wordsworth's *Prelude*, differences in editions may cause trouble. An example of this is the fact that the 1850 *Prelude* (which is very commonly read) contains fourteen books while the 1805 edition consists of thirteen books, and the lines of the two versions, because of modifications in ideas and expression, are differently numbered.

In the presentation of material concerning Wordsworth we have followed the 1805 version of *The Prelude*. For each of the first six books of the poem we have a chapter, and the reader of any of the first six chapters of the present book can turn conveniently to the correspondingly numbered book in the 1805 *Prelude*. Our discussion in almost every instance follows in the same sequence the ideas that are presented in the indicated version of *The Prelude*, and thus parallels are to be found without too much trouble. When a source has been indicated for material drawn from Whitehead, any quotation from him (even in a subsequent paragraph) will be found in the precise page that has been earlier cited, unless the reader is specifically informed otherwise. Any exception to this would be extremely rare.

Something further must be said here about the method that is followed in our general plan. Quotations for the most part will be short, whether from Whitehead or Wordsworth. It will be easy for one to refer to the original sources for more detail. The aim is to reveal the value in reading Whitehead and Wordsworth themselves. Reading about them is not enough. It is important to be able to look back accurately to both figures from time to time. Often the quotation of a single word in Whitehead, especially when followed by a period, will be helpful in finding in the sources the material under discussion. When a line-for-line passage is given from the poet, reference to the number of the first line will appear at the end of the quotation. Short expressions or single words in quotation marks will serve to guide the reader to other passages that are closely related. Thus the whole area in the sources should be readily open to examination. Material in our book will almost invariably follow in sequence material in *The Prelude*. At times when quotation marks are placed around a single word it may seem fussy, but this particular word will aid (it is chosen for that purpose) in tracing ideas expressed in the context of the poet.

There will remain, of course, some problem of personal interpretation of ideas. But the reader should at any rate be able to bring his own personality into a kind of dialogue on the proposed questions of philosophy, or even to provide an invisible censorship of the conclusions that are reached. Thus the reader in a fashion can be a kind of collaborator. The shared work that lies ahead, then, is fittingly referred to as an inquiry. The approach is not that of an assertive declaration with regard to anticipated conclusions, minor or major. Rather, it is that of an interrogation. It asks questions of the various texts in both Wordsworth and Whitehead and receives, so far as it is possible, an answer from the works themselves rather than from any prepossessions.

We have here spoken of method mainly in respect to the handling of the content that is necessary to the study. A further point in regard to method is that, just as in the case of Wordsworth we have drawn material which can be readily verified; so we have also drawn with caution the substance from Whitehead that we need. The aim is, again, that ideas may be readily traced to the evidence on which they are based — in the volumes from which that evidence has been taken. Quotations from Whitehead will be usually short, as we have said, but single words or phrases, we repeat, in quotation marks, will ap-

15

pear in our context to help direct attention to the spot from which the material was taken. The quotation marks around a single word may again (as in single words quoted from Wordsworth) seem fussy, but they have the value of enabling the reader to track Whitehead's ideas conveniently in their context. As in the custom mentioned earlier, other quoted material in a paragraph will be found in the precise place which has been first cited. Indeed, later following quoted material in subsequent paragraphs will be traceable to the same source — unless the context indicates a different one.

From time to time Whitehead will be referred to as "the philosopher," but the expression is not to be taken honorifically. The reference does not hark back to any sense of awe such as that with which Aristotle was regarded by certain thinkers in the Middle Ages. He was then often designated as "the philosopher" as if there had been no other philosopher worth thinking about. Whitehead is deserving of esteem (he has at times been referred to, we may emphasize, as the greatest philosopher of the twentieth century), but the term "the philosopher" will be used only to avoid confusing problems of antecedents or repetitious mention of his name. The same intent applies to the occasional references to Wordsworth as "the poet."

It has been said that the treatment of the subject of the book is to be based on the 1805 *Prelude*. We may add that the 1805 *Prelude* is readily accessible for use, and this version is rather pleasant to read, partly because of the type that has been selected and partly because the edition has a somewhat winning and youthful quality. But to return, now, to the story element that lies ahead. Wordsworth and his poetry will at once be very much in the center of attention. The poet's life is a great story especially in its relation to Whitehead, but our final concern will always be related to philosophy.[11]

We come back now to the subject of peace and community, which had an important place in the thought of both Wordsworth and Whitehead. In our own time this subject has had central significance especially in the socially-oriented philosophy of George Herbert Mead and in the world-view of John Kenneth Galbraith. Mead pointed out that it is a wrong assumption to suppose that the responses of "the West to the East are not comprehensible to each other." [12] We have to awaken, we "are awakening," we may grant, to the importance of a profound insight into *the other* (Buber's term) which we need actually to celebrate. Back of our needs is the necessity of a larger universality in everyone's reflection, whether in the East or West. And celebration or public clarification is not too large a conception for our purpose. Modern public thought is the rude beginning of a dialogue which needs to be enhanced.

Mead conceives of the necessity of working toward the "blessed community" which was also much on the mind of Josiah Royce. John Galbraith has had peace and "The Public State" very much on his conscience for the last decade. He writes on "The Industrial System and the Cold War" [13] and on "The Public State" [14] from a very large and penetrating perspective. He has a recent volume *How to Control the Military* and there is a related topic which is notable in a chapter heading "The Money War" in a 1975 volume, *Money: Whence It Came, Where It Went.* All these things are pertinent to the philosophical problem of peace. Galbraith, indeed, as he thinks of the contradictoriness of the aspects of life, quotes Whitehead in a way which brings out an element of humor: "The beauty of the economic man was that we knew exactly what he was after." [15] It was money. But there was more than humor in Whitehead as we shall see. His economic philosophy, which was part of his larger philosophy, went far beyond the simplistic doctrine of "the economic man," and this is true also of Wordsworth.

*Footnotes*

1. *Science and the Modern World* (New York: Macmillan, 1925, 1937), p. 117.
2. *Ibid.*, p. 112.
3. *Ibid.*, p. 118.
4. *Ibid.*, p. 121.
5. *Ibid.*, p. 5. This principle is followed also by George H. Mead, *Movements of Thought in the Nineteenth Century* (Chicago, 1936, 1950), pp. 25, 54, and 66. See also his concern about mind as communication.
6. *Modes of Thought* (New York: Macmillan, 1938), Capricorn edition, third impression, p. 139. Note the importance of Samuel Alexander's book *Space, Time, and Deity*.
7. *Ibid.*, p. 140.
8. This phrase is from Mead, *The Philosophy of the Present* (La Salle: Open Court, 1959), p. 63, but it applies in a valuable way to Whitehead. Mead's work often provides a useful gloss upon Whitehead.
9. *Science and the Modern World*, p. 285. See also Mead, p. 366, on the problem of how we become selves and "the habits of individuals in their interrelation with each other, the type of habit that is handed down from one generation to another." This quotation from Mead is from *Movements of Thought in the Nineteenth Century*, p. 366.
10. *Ibid.*, p. 121.
11. There is a disparity of one line between the numbering of the lines in Book Nine of the 1805 *Prelude* (London: Oxford University Press, 1936) and in Book Nine of *The Prelude*, published by Oxford in 1960, but material can be readily found and compared in either version of the 1805 poem.
12. *Mind, Self, and Society*, p. 271.
13. This is a chapter heading in *The New Industrial State* (Boston: Houghton Mifflin, 1967), p. 325.

14. Galbraith, *Economics and the Public Purpose* (Boston: Houghton Mifflin, 1973), p. 294.
15. *The New Industrial State*, p. 109. See also "War and the Next Lesson," *Money: Whence It Came* (Boston: Houghton Mifflin, 1975), p. 235, and the chapter "The Ultimate Inflation," p. 146, as well as Galbraith's *How to Control the Military* (Garden City: Doubleday, 1969), p. 55 on "arms industry."

*Chapter I*

# Childhood and School-Time in *The Prelude*: Wordsworth in Relation to Whitehead

Wordsworth's long autobiographical poem *The Prelude* was written almost entirely after 1800 and in its first form gradually came to be planned as a work in five sections. He aimed to survey in the five parts, or books, the early influences of childhood and school that led toward his interest in a career as an exceedingly serious poet. This we plan to trace. Neither the earlier, the short *Prelude*, nor the later long form was originally conceived with the title it finally was given. Nevertheless Wordsworth thought of the work as a prelude or preliminary to other poems — the writing he wished later to produce.

When we say that he had an interest in a career as an exceedingly serious poet we are not using Wordsworth's own ex-

pression about himself. He was not stuffy in this. It was his
hope to reach many readers about concerns which all human
beings have, but the point is that he was not trifling or shallow
about these concerns. For this reason he had even in other
poems tried to work profoundly, connecting, for example,
lyricism to the ballad — working at first on the basis of the
popular ballad — a form of literature which had been earlier
written for and about the people. He was, that is, not simple in
his outlook. Wordsworth's purpose can be conceived best by
saying that he had the aim of being a somewhat philosophical
poet. The word philosophy has reference to his total view,
whereby he would wish to see all that one can in a kind of
togetherness.

In suggesting that Wordsworth planned to approach his new
work philosophically, we are indicating his own and his friend
Coleridge's feeling about the literary tasks that lay ahead.
Wordsworth had been urged toward an interest in philosophy
by Coleridge. We are thinking here of philosophy in a broad
sense, for the two poets themselves thought of it in this way.
And here we may refer to Whitehead, who believed that it is in
the very nature of philosophy to bring orientation and energy
to one's life. This is for him central to the meaning of
philosophy. It has a relation to a person's vital and effective action. In proceeding, we shall see that *The Prelude*, with which
we are here mainly concerned, reflects a point of view
somewhat similar to that of Whitehead.

Wordsworth has long been thought of as a philosophic poet,
but in tracing his thought through *The Prelude* we will see
whether this notion may be adequately validated and perhaps
have a chance to observe in a somewhat new light whatever the
trend of his philosophic thought may be. He has also been
regarded as a "poet-psychologist," or at any rate as a creative
writer who was greatly influenced by the association of ideas
in the psychology of his day. Whitehead, too, had decidedly
psychological interests. Psychology for Wordsworth had, of

course, a bearing on philosophy and this connection was markedly customary in his time. But the main purpose of the present book is to see Wordsworth and Whitehead philosophically in relation to the current day, our own day. In addition to the poet's interest in the association of ideas and in the early psychological concern for "the self," there was the challenge brought to him by the dictum *Know thyself* in the philosopher's sense — which brings us back to what we have earlier implied: that in spite of all the fine work that has already been done on the poet, he may perhaps be better known and understood by approaching his work *The Prelude* somewhat philosophically, in the light of certain problems of a later time, our time. In any case, a great poet always needs to be looked at freshly in every age — in view of changes that are occurring in a new world.

Is Wordsworth a great poet? Could he be great without being philosophical? He has at times been regarded as the greatest English poet of his period, and those who hold this view would probably extend such a time-limit to include the entire nineteenth century and part of the twentieth. With this extended scope in mind, we can look back for a moment to a portion of an earlier period preceding Wordsworth's and try to judge his greatness as compared, say, to that of Alexander Pope. However one may value literary men in various ages, Wordsworth remains a figure to reckon with beyond a single century. The present book may help the reader of it in such a tentative evaluation, and all such evaluations must necessarily remain hypothetical. Wordsworth, at any rate, is a poet who, as we have said, sought to face the problem *Know thyself*.

Psychology which like philosophy is involved in knowing the self had for Wordsworth a meaning somewhat different from what it has today. As he turned back to examine his earliest experiences psychologically, however, he was following a procedure that twentieth-century psychology has often employed in attempting to understand personal development through various stages. He wished, that is, to know *himself* better through a psychological and philosophical analysis in so far as it was possible. To this end he wished to turn even to his earliest recollections, and he hoped to understand better something of the complexities of the mature personality. But his purpose also was to make himself known more completely to his closest friend, Coleridge. His work contains a kind of personalism. Ultimately it was his wish to share his life with others and thus to project his existence beyond himself. For the immediate present, however, he felt that the one person he knew who would understand this purpose most fully would be his close friend who was likewise concerned about the growth of a poet's inner nature. The poem was therefore addressed to Coleridge. All this is brought out in the course of successive pages in *The Prelude*.

Wordsworth's earliest recollections, as we have said, play an important part in the poem. But since he has in view a purpose other than sheer narration, he does not at once present remembrances of his childhood. We refer now to the beginning of *The Prelude*. As he considers the work of the moment, his writing, he wants his main theme, that of joy — profound joy — to be dominant. In the course of the poem he is to present moments of seriousness, regret, sadness, even melancholy; but these he feels are not the main moods that give to the reader what is most deeply needed or desired. There is a kind of potential reader-interest, therefore, in the fact that the work begins in joy and gives promise of being constructive in its substance. We are all interested in joy. As the poem continues it will emphasize the author's complete faith in life. His philosophy represents a kind of anti-pessimism. This is a part of his positive philosophy, or world-view.

Such a faith in life can become for the modern reader in our age of so-called anxiety — or indeed for any reader in any period — one of the poem's most exhilarating features. It is by no means a tragic work — though a poem which is tragic can of

23

course also be exhilarating. As we think of *The Prelude* we may consider a profound sense of the word "Comedy" which Dante applies to his own greatest work. Both *The Prelude* and Dante's poem are aimed at an ending characterized by joy but in different ways. Can joy be philosophic? Distresses and tragedies that Wordsworth suffers are touched upon for the purpose of showing how he surmounted them in daily living or in reflection. His continuing existence itself carried with it inevitable growth, he feels, and reflection has brought him added rewards. This also we see illustrated in *The Prelude*.

A breeze of surprising freshness blows through the opening pages of the poem where Wordsworth describes himself on a journey seeking a home. Wherever he may decide to settle and live he is convinced there will be abundant reason to have confidence that his life work will be successfully pursued. The whole world in its totality is his study; it is the abiding place of his essential life. It is not a destructive world, as some men have believed. This total creation is generously open to him. Even a twig in a stream he says — speaking in hyperbole — could give him direction: he could safely follow *many* of the different paths available, or indicated to him by signs of nature, and could still reach his true destination successfully. In Wordsworth's view, beneficent cosmic forces work upon all men. The creative universe blows its breath from without upon him — as well as upon all humanity and he has

> felt within
> A corresponding mild creative breeze ... (42—)

This inner factor is important. Wordsworth moves beyond a philosophy of externalism. The inwardness of each person — the "me" in contrast to the great outer world of the "not-me" — possesses its profound character. It acts as a complementary cosmic force, scarcely less dynamic — so at least it seems in this highly personal view — than the external one. The word

24

"mild" in this passage should not mislead the reader into thinking that this is an impotent breeze. The wind which caresses him from the fields is gentle and kindly (Wordsworth emphasizes this at the moment), and the other creative breath from within is likewise beneficent in its potentialities. In bringing a benefit to him it reveals that it can be similarly beneficial to all human beings. The poet shows humility, as may be seen in reading this passage of *The Prelude* and in examining many others. But paradoxically it is not a humility that would prevent him from writing for others a psychological epic on his entire spirit's history.

In speaking earlier of Wordsworth's complete faith in life (and in suggesting it here by allusions to material in *The Prelude*) we might have illustrated at once a relationship between his thought and that of Whitehead. That confidence in the potentialities which life may bring has been evident from the first, and it may recall to one's mind a parallel in that Whitehead, while explaining the meaning of philosophy as he sees it, suggests that it brings one "a sense of the worth of life" and is in addition an energizing force which contributes to "effort." [1] Here the philosopher explains the kind of effort he has in mind, for he refers to it as "civilized effort." Likewise in Wordsworth what is occurring is a kind of self-civilization which can be a possible end-product as he reflects upon action that lies ahead. Philosophy can help one to aspire to an intentionality: to things which without such spiritual perception he might never dream of achieving. The dream can in itself be an inspiring aid to mankind. It can help one to face fear which, if faced, can, as Plato says, lead one to courage.

Why are we sometimes *afraid* to proceed toward action? Wordsworth wonders about the question: Why do we have fears and in what sense are they, or are they not, surmountable? Are fears important? Do they form a part of human growth? The problem of action was tremendously important to Wordsworth and to Whitehead also — as well as to William

James, whom Whitehead greatly admired. It was, moreover, important to Dewey, toward whom, in addition, Whitehead felt a very considerable respect. William James, speaking as a psychologist — though of course he was a philosopher as well — once pointed out that when we are afraid, and we run, it may be that we are really most afraid *because* we run. Always it is true also that in the midst of life's problems we may *hide* — or indeed perhaps hide our heads in the sand.

But according to William James if we rush toward a necessary danger with the idea of fighting rather than fleeing we may find ourselves becoming strangely more courageous. We shall have occasion to return later to the problem of action and of the self, but there is a kind of invisible red badge that we can have the honor of possessing silently. When we act, or run toward necessary danger, and in doing so become more courageous, this change within the self, we may say, is partly because we run toward our responsibility. Acting out a role has been frequently considered by modern psychologists as a stage in defining the self. Somewhat similarly, Wordsworth discovered that his first words in certain early passages of *The Prelude* cheered him as he spontaneously put them into poetical form. But he tells us that he was aided "far more" by

> the mind's
> Internal echo of the imperfect sound . . . (64—)

What is this internal "echo" of the physical or "imperfect" sound? It is clearly something intangible. For Wordsworth this abstract echo was cheering: It served as a reminder of still finer things that he could undoubtedly accomplish in the future. Self-consciousness often troubles a person when he first sits down to write. But it is not in a state of nervous agitation or self-conscious literary creation that Wordsworth would now be about his task. There was a confidence and conviction that permitted him to relax for a moment. Does a writer relax at his work or does he make an attack which is at once formidably energetic?

Doubtless in writing there may be a combination of momentary peaceful relaxing and meditating, as well as spurts of energetic driving which move one forward. Wordsworth, at any rate decides to lie down beneath a tree in leisurely fashion to let "many thoughts" pass through his mind, almost as chance leads them. Can this be philosophic? He is relaxed. This may at times be a desirable state for any writer. Let the internal activity, that is, proceed in its process. For the present his method of approach is that of reverie. There is a sense of ease and freedom in his introspection. In this he is perhaps something like the creative Rousseau, to whom he has been often compared in a variety of ways? Is he, however, more philosophic than Rousseau?

There is a danger that the comparison between Wordsworth and Rousseau may be made superficially. Wordsworth well knew what serious labor meant, and perhaps Rousseau also was well aware of certain kinds of rigor involved in creativity. But now we may mention that Wordsworth, like Rousseau, had sympathy for the state of mind of the peasant. After leaving the tree, and his relaxation, he proceeds on his way with a sense of identification with the humbler classes which appears in the statement:

> So like a Peasant I pursued my road
> Beneath the evening sun ... (110—)

Wordsworth identifies to a very considerable extent with all classes of human beings. Is this philosophic? In the line we have just quoted he uses capitalization in the word "Peasant," and he does so probably for the purpose of emphasis, as often seems to be the case in his writing. Whitehead also is concerned about human beings at all levels. It is, he says, the effect of masses of people which needs to be remembered most importantly in any social movement — when we consider "the general direction of society,"[2] though criticism which provides a "precise aim" in one way or another is of course given most importantly by great individuals. In this connection he emphasizes later the fact that among the masses a variety of "conditions may prevent certain types of talent" from arriving at "fruition"; the span of time and space and locality need to be considered in making any estimate about these things concerning the status of persons. As to Wordsworth, there is a further suggestion of the Rousseau-like mood that he establishes when he refers to

> The admiration and the love, the life
> In *common* things . . . (117—)

We have added italics to emphasize the fact that here also there seems to be a connection with Rousseau. Delight in imagination is another factor that connects the two men. The general spirit of an attitude toward human beings is, however, the main concern in this portion of *The Prelude*. It appears, for example, when Wordsworth mentions certain poetical themes that come to his mind in his strolling — themes that represent possibilities for his own future poetry, among them —

> some old
> Romantic tale, by Milton left unsung . . . (179—)

The themes of romance served as a source for one of the aspects of the period of which Wordsworth was a part, and it was natural that he should think of their offering a possibility for his own use. As he anticipates the future there is the open field of some subject drawn from chivalry. He is dreaming about this as a possibility. Undoubtedly it is the idealist element in such themes that attracts him. Chivalry is important to philosophy. Here we can think of the prominent place of medieval chivalry in the early stages of the making of the mind of modern man; that is, the ideal of chivalry contributes spiritually even to the period in which Wordsworth lived, and his period in turn importantly contributes to ours. Whitehead, too, appreciates values of social cohesion and togetherness which have come down to us from the Middle Ages and expresses his indebtedness to the work of Henry Osborn Taylor, especially an indebtedness to Taylor's *The Medieval Mind*.[3]

Surveying various other epic possibilities, apart from the medieval, Wordsworth comes to a subject of tragic nature concerning the character of Sertorius, a Roman general of the first century. In this story, which the poet projects as he is imaginatively conceiving it, what is most vital to the mind of man is never, he believes, to be lost. The soul remains free, can always be free. The most vital thing is, it would seem, to know yourself: to know where *you* are personally. This is a part of the know-thyself doctrine. In the story there would be a long process of cultural destruction surrounding the hero, but spiritual devastation would not be the final theme of the work. Wordsworth's attitude here is not negative. Freedom would still be dominant. It is the soul which is the ultimate source for mankind in creative living as also in the creative life. Arts and laws may gradually die out among men

> but not the Soul
> Of Liberty . . . (195—)

Thus far it is the personal within the individual soul that has mainly seemed attractive to Wordsworth, but social problems also present themselves dynamically within his mind. There is a reverence, not only for the self. Self-reverence can show reverence for every other self — it can be human in humaneness. The doctrine *know-thyself* should be understood within a frame of thought which includes social problems, as, for example, in our own day in Mead and Chardin. In Wordsworth they are present, for example, when, in continuing his thought about epic themes, he comes to that great lover of civil

29

and religious liberty, Gustavus I of Sweden. Wandering among the workers in the midlands of his country, clothed as a lowly laborer, Gustavus

> found
> Help at his need in Dalecarlia's Mines ... (211—)

A king's eagerness to take on a humble role in the time of his country's dire need — this is a subject close to Wordsworth's heart. If we think of him as a poet with somewhat philosophical interests it is as a humanist philosopher in the modern sense that we must to a very large extent consider him — a humanist who is greatly concerned with problems of justice and of humanity here on earth. In certain appreciative comments Whitehead himself notes the poet Wordsworth's vital interest in society, along with his concern for man and nature generally. [4]

As Wordsworth lingers over the possible themes he does not move in a straight line, but is he moving in curves that are useful? We may feel that anyone who has so many subjects to dwell upon must lack something in the way of personal focus; perhaps he has no subject sensibly in mind. Is he like a whirligig beetle? This criticism of him has a certain validity — or at least plausibility — for Wordsworth displays himself as one who knows irresolution common to all people, but most especially common to the immature: for example, to adolescents who may be trying to be writers. There is a melancholia, almost despair, that attends such irresolution. Can a philosopher be humble? The author acknowledges that he is a victim of the psychology of one who proceeds

> with no skill to part
> Vague longing that is bred of want of power
> From paramount impulse not to be withstood ...
> (247—)

Wordsworth confesses frankly, then, that irresolution has been an essential part of his experience — in his actual writing and in his own life. The philosophy of will and of intentionality is a problem here. Such a philosophy realizes the danger, or at times evil, of intention that becomes non-intention or that moves about in blind circles. But now the problem for the poet is how to overcome the danger: how to gain what even in the Middle Ages and later had been called intentionality. Indeed, Wordsworth says, one might "better never to have heard" about "zeal or just ambition" if one is to be confused by a consciousness that repeatedly

> Turns recreant to her task, takes heart again,
> Then feels immediately some hollow thought
> Hang like an interdict upon her hopes. (260—)

Wordsworth, it may have been sensed earlier, is a poet who has guilt feelings, and there may be various sources of such emotions in any person. Sometimes, indeed, the sense of guilt is a part of one's culture, fostered by an unfortunate absoluteness that certain cults attempt to impose (and very largely succeed in imposing) as a doctrine which, they hold, must be submitted to by the human race. This may not be true essence of the religion, but it is difficult to escape an enveloping social atmosphere of this kind. But Wordsworth was chiefly influenced by a more hopeful tradition in human thought. The freedom of certain philosophies and of the Quaker religion, and of some other religions, which left a wide area to the individual's personal thought and experience, was becoming prevalent in the region of England surrounding, and especially to the east of, the place of Wordsworth's birth. But even supposing Quaker or other forms of independency not to have been an influence upon the poet's thought, there is a notable high seriousness and dedication in a great variety of religions which might cause guilt feelings of various kinds. At any rate, Wordsworth, after giving us the lines in *The Prelude* which we have last quoted, goes on to confess that it has been his "lot" as a creative writer to see imperfections in his chosen themes or of seeing

> of absolute accomplishment
> Much wanting, so much wanting, in myself,
> That I recoil and droop, and seek repose,
> In listlessness from vain perplexity,
> Unprofitably travelling toward the grave,
> Like a false steward who hath much received
> And renders nothing back. (265—)

It becomes increasingly evident that Wordsworth's theme in *The Prelude* concerns very largely his problems not only as a man, but as a writer. Can writing, can expression be a part of philosophy? From his introduction of this theme concerning writing he turns to a consideration of the opportunities for health and growth that were available to him in childhood and in his early school time; later he treats of his university days and his experience abroad. Now, as he writes, he feels that the good fortune he has had should shame his recreant spirit. Illustrating his childhood feelings there are passages widely known, though not very familiar philosophically, such as the famous lines beginning

> Fair seed-time had my soul, and I grew up
> Foster'd alike by beauty and by fear ... (305—)

Wordsworth, in this passage, brings together beauty and fear — which may seem to be strangely juxtaposed — as instrumentalities in the nurturing of a human being. The emphasis of an element of fear may lead us to wonder again whether an imposed dogma may be influencing him: the idea of a *dreaded* God. As opposed to such a conception (of a fear-inspiring superpower acting according to caprice) there is the conception of a

32

noncapricious world, or a universe of law. This view, stressing law, is not necessarily inconsistent with belief in the existence of a God. The view that Whitehead, for example, accepts — and that, as he believes, the history of humanity is pointing toward — is that of a non-vengeant order; it involves at a minimum "some measure of regularity, or of persistence or recurrence" [5] in the very nature of the universe.

The idea of a universe of law comes to more or less primitive mankind as a welcome relief from an earlier sense of insecurity within which the human being lives. In speaking of those earlier ages, Whitehead remarks that we as human beings are influenced by "legends, weird, horrible, beautiful, expressing in curious, specialized ways the interweaving of law and capriciousness in the mystery of things. It is the problem of good and evil." He goes on to explain that, in the history of man, for the elementary, early-day thinker, "Sometimes the law is good and the capriciousness evil"; on the other hand, the law itself may seem "iron and evil" and the idea of intervention by a capricious God may appear "merciful and good." Relatively primitive thought attributes personality to certain aspects of causation which in the more advanced stages of civilization humanity regards as neutral — or as based on no conscious intent. Wordsworth, it seems, is seeking an explanation of personal fear, but not necessarily on any dogmatic basis. Fear can be a part of philosophy.

The child in his development may be faced with the same problem of fear that Whitehead mentions. At any rate Wordsworth, like Whitehead, looks for an explanation of fear whereby a sense of one's being at home in the universe will be retained. Fear will be an inevitable part of our life — it can have a constructive side even in regard to the sense of the mystery which surrounds us. As Wordsworth brings together both beauty and fear, the juxtaposition of these forces tends to mitigate the most baleful aspects of the latter of the two factors. Fear is rarely an uncompounded emotion. It has its connections with the mysterious, as well as with reverence. One can also have a sense (in no cowardly way) of a fear that one may do a wrong, a fear which may be compounded with a desire to take a proper place in connection with various constructive actions, and on this basis it is possible that one may resolutely proceed toward something which is not a mere blind destiny. The poet explains that he had a conviction, even in youth, of the reality of something beyond that of the world of matter and motion. Nature must be understood as more than a thing of mere physical occurrences. Thus far there is a parallel in the thought of Wordsworth to that of Whitehead, whose attacks on materialism are frequent. As Whitehead views philosophy itself, "It is the architect of the buildings of the spirit . . . and the spiritual precedes the material." [7] Fear has a place in some idealistic or other kinds of philosophies.

When Wordsworth regards nature as something more than a matter of mere physical occurrences he does so through a kind of intuitive sense which he has of the spiritual in the world. In a particular period of his boyhood he was more than once guilty of a theft about which he was later profoundly unhappy, and on a certain moonlit night after he had stolen a boat he heard "low breathings" behind his shoulder and sounds of "motion," though he could not tell what was pursuing him. Wordsworth believes, it seems, that there is something like conscience — an urge toward goodness and justice, not revealed authoritatively to us it is true, but implicitly present in the cosmos. He feels decidedly an awareness of spiritual forces. As he climbed a cliff on one of his rambles, the sky above him "seemed not a sky" of the world as he had known the world in everyday experience; the clouds appeared to be animated by something cosmic, not by mere wind. Thinking of the making of mind, or soul, Wordsworth is struck by the interaction that takes place between sense-data, so-called, and something which he feels is not immediately evident to sense, but is in a mysterious way perceptible.

Here it may be helpful to recall certain remarks of

Whitehead with reference to the intuitive side of man — for example, a passage pointing out emphatically at the outset of a paragraph that "Human life is driven forward by its dim apprehension of notions too general for its existing language. Such ideas cannot be grasped singly, one by one in isolation." [8] The reason for this difficulty is that the process by which "mankind advances in its apprehension of the general nature of things" [9] is slow; we grasp specifics such as the shapes of the leaves of the yellow oak, or of a hard maple, or of a particular poplar tree, but the broadly reaching conceptions (such as the idea of democracy in Mexico and in France) enter our minds in some degree of confused and imperfect ascertainment. The individual very gradually apprehends in what respects groups of ideas are "elucidating each other."

The development of thought in the individual or in the race, Whitehead says, comes largely through the advance of such apprehension. "It is the task of philosophy to promote this growth in mentality." [10] More explicitly, there is reference elsewhere in Whitehead's volume to "our direct intuitions which we enjoy prior to all verbalization" — as well as to "our literary modes of verbal expression," [11] which are closely related to such symbolic intuitions. "The chief danger in philosophy," he goes on to say, "is that the dialectic deductions from inadequate formulae" at times "exclude direct intuitions" [12] from receiving explicit attention. These "direct intuitions" *are* a subtle perceptivity.

We have spoken of the importance of knowing oneself as being related to the very meaning of philosophy. But it may well be re-emphasized that knowing oneself is not an entirely inward condition. We scarcely exist if we think of ourselves as unrelated to others. And knowing the self also requires strength and personal control, as well as continued effort at self-education, which is not a matter of doing only the things that to the self seem personally interesting. Reverence, not merely of the self, is a part of all this. Thus, to come back to Whitehead, his feeling of the importance of reverence appears even in his attitude toward education. A truly fine education, in the view of the philosopher we are speaking of, should include something within its essence which is religious. It should include the attainment of the very spirit of "reverence." [13] And ethics is also a part of it.

For Whitehead "the foundation of reverence is this perception, that the present holds within itself the complete sum of existence, backwards and forwards, that whole amplitude of time, which is eternity." These words appear in a very emphatic position, as the climax to a chapter in the book from which we have been quoting. They embrace something of ethics which goes beyond the simple training which is given to the person as a child within his own family. Norman Kemp Smith, as has been indicated, relates fear to reverence. Thus he refers to the fact that the expression *reverence for God* has been, in substance, substituted for fear in a certain Biblical translation.[14] The original word for fear, that is, before translation, means reverence.

Knowing oneself then, or thinking philosophically, includes reverence and intuition. Especially in our own modern age we need, when we think philosophically, to recognize the extreme variability of people. This Whitehead himself stresses in his most mature writing by referring to a need for "deeper knowledge of the varieties of human nature" [15] — something which we rarely sufficiently consider. Explaining in brief what the term philosophy means, Whitehead says later, "Philosophy is at once general and concrete, critical and appreciative of direct intuition." [16] And in the page following that from which we have just quoted he again relates philosophy to the necessity of "reverence," and shortly thereafter to a serious concern and respect for others. Thus, as we think of the term philosophy we observe that the matter of philosophy is expansive in the sense that it expands steadily in our social perceptions as the attempt is made to study it.

We have seen that poetry may provide, as Whitehead sug-

36

gests, the direct intuitions that philosophy might exclude from attention. Wordsworth, for example, points out that elements which apparently are discordant find harmonization in the processes by which a human being undergoes inward growth, the attaining of an inwardness that is derived from our inorganic and animal forebears. We may recall the seemingly animistic side of the poet's allusions to the inorganic world and also to the world of vegetation. All bodies, all objects, it seems, have a kind of perception. Here we may also cite the fact that Whitehead refers appreciatively to a non-passive line of thought in a statement by Francis Bacon which goes as follows: "It is certain that all bodies whatsoever, though they have no sense, yet have perception . . . for when one body is applied to another, there is a kind of election to embrace that which is agreeable, and to exclude or to expel that which is ingrate. . . ." 17

Shortly afterward, having quoted Bacon, Whitehead goes on to say that Bacon in this statement is "outside the physical line of thought which finally dominated" the seventeenth century. In the later stages of the seventeenth century (and in the eighteenth century) there was frequently a physical tendency to stress "passive matter which was operated on externally by forces." Whitehead adds that he believes the non-passive "line of thought" indicated in Bacon expresses "more fundamental truth than do the materialistic concepts which were then being shaped as adequate for physics." If this non-passive "line of thought" was more adequate for the future development of physics than the view which emphasizes "passive matter," we can see how Whitehead's philosophy (which is friendly to the non-passive emphasis) has a connection with Wordsworth's conceptions.

We have referred to the relations between man and the inorganic, as well as to the vegetable and the animal base which is antecedent to him. One should notice here Wordsworth's use of animal imagery for his poetical purposes. In the winter the boy and his friends, skating on the ice, were a 'Pack loud bellowing," and there are other examples of animal imagery that he uses in exhibiting the physical spirits displayed in boyhood life. We may observe also the poet's use of capitalization (in the animal-like word "Pack"); he is probably here and — as we have suggested — elsewhere employing capitalization for the purpose of emphasis.

Acceptance of the universe — inorganic, animal, and human — is characteristic of the poet, but it is not a passive acquiescence; it appears side by side with individual activity. Nevertheless, apart from this type of acquiescence, fear likewise makes its contribution to the boy's development. Fear has seemed for him to be not only related to beauty but to be almost a part of beauty in and of itself. It is manifested in the experience of beauty. It is, moreover, a part of the experience of morality. The cliff or peak above him as he rowed on Esthwaite Water at night — as seen from an unusual perspective — *strode* symbolically after him. His brain, at the same time,

> Work'd with a dim and undetermin'd sense
> Of unknown modes of being ... (419—)

So, he tells us, he was fed through his own experience — and not dogmatically — with feelings of the spiritual and the natural, for very early he was developing a rudimentary philosophy concerning the elemental forces at work in the world. Even at this young age (he is looking back to his boyhood when he was perhaps fourteen), he was not following in slavish, mechanical fashion the position enunciated by any other person — whether teacher, rector, or friend; what he was seeking was nothing merely repetitive which lacked meaning to him inwardly. He was, that is, doing a thing which was his own. For Wordsworth, the operation of the unconscious was obviously an important factor. In his thoughts there was a "darkness," and he tells us

> huge and mighty Forms that do not live
> Like living men mov'd slowly through the mind
> By day and were the trouble of my dreams ... (425—)

All of these things, though connected with fear, he regarded
as gifts to him, granted with unstinted "kindness"; they were
gifts whether in the time of November, with "vapours rolling
down the valleys" which contributed to the loneliness of the
scene something which was even "more lonesome," and they
were likewise gifts to him in summer when he went homeward
"beneath the gloomy hills" in solitude. Discordant elements of
fear and joy were thus reconciled, as he tells us, by an "invisible workmanship." Through all his experience, as it is recorded, runs a multiple associationism

> and thus
> By the impressive discipline of fear,
> By pleasure and repeated happiness,
> So frequently repeated, and by force
> Of obscure feeling representative
> Of joys that were forgotten, these same scenes,
> So beauteous and majestic in themselves,
> Though yet the day was distant, did at length
> Become habitually dear ... (630—)

Wordsworth's treatment of his early life in Book One of *The
Prelude* (which Whitehead greatly admired) — including as
this passage shows his interest in associationism — does not
represent a materialistic or mechanical type of the association-
of-ideas doctrine which in various periods has been prevalent.
Now we may mention that the poet's presentation of his life
during his youth may be related to the analysis of a similar
period in which Whitehead speaks of youth's "whole-hearted

absorption in personal enjoyments and personal discomforts." [18] This is a special period of "pleasure and quick pain, quick laughter and quick tears, quick absence of care, and quick diffidence, quick courage and quick fear" — which may be seen as "conjointly characters of youth." Whitehead goes on to say that this time in life "is too chequered to be termed a happy period. It is vivid rather than happy." But for Wordsworth, though his life too had its darks and lights, youth was a time mainly of joy. Nevertheless he would doubtless agree with Whitehead's words, "Youth is not peaceful in any ordinary sense of that term." But it is a time of being very much alive, in the sense that is suggested as an incidental overtone in Whitehead's repetition of the word "quick"; it is a time, also, that helps to make us what we are and that contributes to the building of our philosophy, whatever that philosophy may be.

Whitehead, like Wordsworth, alludes to the animal aspect of young human beings, though he carries this further than does the poet. Perhaps the philosopher is closer to reality in this respect than is Wordsworth. But Whitehead does point out that apart from the self-orientation of a person in this early period, youth's "very search for personal experience" also "elicits impersonality, self-forgetfulness." [19] Thus in time youth can pass "from selfishness to devotion." Further, after "youth has once grasped where Beauty dwells — with a real knowledge and not as a mere matter of literary phraseology in some poetic, scriptural, or psychological version . . . its self-surrender is absolute. The vision may pass. It may traverse consciousness in a flash." But youth is the time when the vision usually comes, and it may lead, it should naturally lead, to a philosophy in which one seeks the higher peace, a "harmony of the soul's activities with ideal aims. . . ." This harmony Wordsworth also sought.

The poet's first purpose in recounting his "spirit's history" is, as we have said, to know himself. This was a large task — as he well realized when he suggested to his friend Coleridge that his effort might not be successful:

> Yet should these hopes
> Be vain, and thus should neither I be taught
> To understand myself, nor thou to know
> With better knowledge how the heart was fram'd
> Of him thou lovest, need I dread from thee
> Harsh judgments, if I am so loth to quit
> Those recollected things, and lovely forms
> And sweet sensations that throw back our life
> And almost make our Infancy itself
> A visible scene, on which the sun is shining (653—)

Wordsworth had small need to fear judgments which were "harsh" from Coleridge, to whom he was presenting as a gift this study of that inner, expansive, personal psychology with which they were both fascinated because of its importance to humanity. These poets together, like Whitehead later, were greatly drawn to the analysis of childhood and youth — in a word, they were attracted to what they would call the soul's development — and with it the analysis of all inner psychology in relation to the universe and the individual's stages of being. Whitehead, similarly concerned, feels that a dynamism is present in the processes which bring about these stages. Could Wordsworth have been somewhat aware of the stages of the dynamic processes?

We have said in the "Biographical Summary" that when the poet was a student at Cambridge, mathematics was taught in a manner approximately one hundred years behind the times. The instruction had not reached much beyond the 1689-1699 period of Newton.

But Newton's "fluents" and "fluxions" were potent; they were tremendous ideas. They concerned a flowing action and variations in movement, for example in a mathematical curve. The "fluxions" were derivatives, or rates of change. We have incidentally pointed out that Wordsworth had a sense of the potential dynamism within the movement, or the flowing action, of a wheel. This dynamism is to some extent evident in his short poem "Written in Very Early Youth."

Wordsworth from his earliest stages was in the main quiet and reflective, but he was far from static in his point of view. For him, as for Whitehead, life is a movement, a passage from mystery to mystery. It is no fixed thing. Even in its moments of quietness it suggests the possibility of transformations that are potent: and transformation may be seen in space and time as incipient force-in-motion. We have referred to the potential dynamism which may be thought of as being present in a wheel, in view of its design for the purpose of motion. Things broadly speaking, are in process, and they are characterized by interrelation.

The poem "Written in Early Youth" makes reference to the calmness in the wheel, but allusively there is present the potential, the nonstatic quality which a "resting wheel" possesses, especially if we are thinking of the gigantic wheel-like movements of the planets and stars in the universe, which Wordsworth has here in mind. We can see something of this kind of dynamism, in a different way, in another poem, "It Is a Beauteous Evening," which was written in 1802, in the period in which he was writing *The Prelude*. In this poem he refers to the "holy time" which is "quiet as a Nun" in her moment of utmost adoration. A kind of timelessness in "time" of the whole universe is likened to the moment which the nun is experiencing as Wordsworth views her. The word "calm" appears in the work as it does in the poem which has reference to the "resting wheel"; this along with Wordsworth's haunting allusions to the child who lies "in Abraham's bosom" throughout the year — recalling the sixteenth chapter of Luke and suggesting a sense of time and eternity — gives us a feeling for the spiritually dynamic which is symbolized further, or is reinforced, in the image of the unsleeping sea.

It is interrelation, then, which is involved here. Things are not in any sense static or isolated. They are connected. Words-worth's position is somewhat parallel to that of Whitehead when, for example, the philosopher criticizes separateness and materialism. As a forerunner in regard to Wordsworth's and Whitehead's conceptions about separateness and materialism we could think of various developmental philosophers, among them Immanuel Kant, famous for his comments on judgment. In Kant's view we cannot understand a point in space unless we conceive it as a limit. The point is something we can *approach*, but we can never bag it as we can bag an apple or a walnut. Its relationships to other things are what we need to perceive. The position of interrelation does, then, appear in Kant. It can be seen in a passage which Whitehead, in his chapter on "Relativity," quotes from Kant as follows: "Time and space are quanta continua, because there is no part of them that is not enclosed between limits (points and moments), *no part that is not itself again a space or a time.* " [20] The fluent or flowing quality of time as well as space is here being emphasized. The importance of this will appear in material later to be presented.

Near the close of Book One of *The Prelude* Wordsworth, we have said, addresses Coleridge with reference to "judgments" of the poem, harsh or otherwise, that might be made. These poets were both greatly attracted to the problems of change in childhood and youth: in a word, the problems of development. They were concerned with the analysis of an inner psychology in relation to the wider universe and man's stages of being. The modern world has gone beyond them in this, under the influence of William James and Freud. But Wordsworth and Coleridge prepare the way for a variety of later developments. Our life is marked by expansiveness. We have been fascinated today with childhood and the need for an analysis of it because of its cultural and practical importance to older individuals and mankind. The expansiveness in Wordsworth, and in his poetry, is an expansiveness inward and in depth, which will be further examined in the next chapter.

43

## Footnotes

1. *Adventures of Ideas* (New York: Macmillan, 1933, 1949), p. 125. Compare also Pierre Teilhard de Chardin, *The Future of Man* (New York: Harper and Row, 1964), p. 213.
2. *Dialogues of Alfred North Whitehead*, recorded by Lucien Price (Boston: Atlantic Monthly, Little, Brown and Co., second printing, 1954), p. 120.
3. *Adventures of Ideas*, p. vii.
4. *Science and the Modern World* (New York: Macmillan, 1937), p. 118. Whitehead shows that Wordsworth deliberately aimed to write a philosophical poem containing views of society, as well as views on nature and man generally.
5. *Adventures of Ideas*, p. 139. See also Norman Kemp Smith's interpretation of Whitehead and of fear, *The Credibility of Divine Existence* (New York: Macmillan, St. Martin's Press, 1967), p. 226 and p. 417. Reverence is a factor of Smith's view of fear.
6. *Ibid.*, p. 141.
7. *Science and the Modern World*, p. x. See also p. 157 for references to "the materialist theory" and the reduction to "matter."
8. *Adventures of Ideas*, p. 29.
9. *Ibid.*, p. 30.
10. *Ibid.*, p. 30.
11. *Ibid.*, p. 177.
12. *Ibid.*, pp. 177-178.
13. *The Aims of Education* (New York: Macmillan, 1929, 1966), p. 23. Smith, referred to earlier, connects fear closely with reverence. Fear has a place in Smith's philosophy. See *The Credibility of Divine Existence*, p. 430 for references to Wordsworth.
14. Smith, p. 423, footnote, refers to Moffatt's substitution

"for the traditional translation of Ps. CXI. 10 — 'Fear of the Lord is the beginning of wisdom' — 'The first thing in knowledge is reverence for the Eternal.' "

15. *Adventures of Ideas*, p. 120.
16. *Ibid.*, p. 125. Whitehead's concern for others, under the term "respect," appears on p. 127 where he refers to "sympathy, and general kindliness."
17. Bacon, as quoted in *Science and the Modern World*, pp. 60-61.
18. *Adventures of Ideas*, p. 370.
19. *Ibid.*, p. 371.
20. *Science and the Modern World*, p. 184. Whitehead is here quoting from *The Critique of Pure Reason*. The italics are Whitehead's. Kant at times does make statements that are inconsistent with interrelationism.

## Chapter II

# *The Prelude*
# and Later School Days
# of Wordsworth as
# Related to Whitehead's
# Thought

Near the outset of the last chapter mention was made of the fact that *The Prelude*, Wordsworth's autobiographical poem, was written almost in its entirety after 1800 and it was at first planned as a work to be completed in five sections. The first section, or book, was to deal with his childhood and early school days. The second section — or Wordsworth's Book Two of *The Prelude* — is to be covered in the present chapter, which will consist of a continuation of what the poet called "School-Time," covering the period preparatory to his experience at Cambridge University. As Wordsworth opens this section he addresses his friend, Coleridge, and tells of the "round of tumult" which he and his schoolfellows enjoyed "till daylight fail'd," by which time the cloud in the sky was "edged with twinkling stars" and all the laborers of the community had long since fallen asleep. When the young Wordsworth and his youthful companions found their way to their beds, their "joints" were weary and their minds were still reverberating from their evening's activities.

But with all the boisterousness of such a period, the time had nevertheless come when there was a requirement of further development beyond the violence or over-reacting in very young boyhood. Wordsworth now needed, he suggests, a growth leading to something other than youthful hostility, with its attendant competition, greed, and ruthlessness. What he is leading toward is a new stage in *relatedness*: the appreciation of pleasures characterized by something more nearly approaching calmness and peace. An effective expression of the ruthless mood of his younger days appears in a poem which was originally written as a part of *The Prelude*, but which he decided to publish separately, under the title "Nutting," in 1800. In it he portrays the buccaneering tendency of acquisitiveness or self-aggrandizement which is common in youth — a kind of boyish counterpart of the rape of the frontier going on in new continents across the seas.

The self-centered youth who is given portrayal, after his "merciless ravage" which included the unnecessary breaking of huge boughs from the tree he had attacked, finally pauses and thinks. He looks up with sorrow at the great spaces among the leaves through which the sky can peer. He has come to feel that there is a spirit in the forest that has been desecrated by his destructiveness. So, too, in *The Prelude* Wordsworth pictures a group of boys who are rowing together on Windermere and who compete in a fashion which could easily give rise to feelings of inferiority in the losers and stimulate vainglory in the pride of strength, or of skill, in the conquerors. The goal, or "the selected bourne," in the rowing competition

47

Was now an Island musical with birds
That sang for ever; now a Sister Isle
Beneath the oaks' umbrageous covert, sown
With lilies of the valley, like a field . . . (59—)

The beauty of the lilies in the one island and the overpower-
ing song of the birds on another stand in contrast with the
animal spirits displayed in the competition that the boys had
carried on. Here there is a beauty that modifies or tempers the
seeming insensitivity which the youths show at moments — for
example, in their rough competitiveness. Response to such
beauty modifies, or tempers, the cruder impulses of human beings. As an outgrowth of this tempering factor, the personal in-
dependence that finally accrues is deep rather than superficial;
victory in sports, Wordsworth feels, need not result in attitudes
of self-aggrandizement. In the poem he is promoting the same
spirit of *sharing*, the one-world spirit, that appears elsewhere in
his work, and that is exemplified in Coleridge's poem "The Ancient Mariner," to which Wordsworth contributed by offering
discussion with reference to the theme and by writing some
lines for the actual work. As Wordsworth says of the contest in
which the boys participated

In such a race,
So ended, disappointment could be none,
Uneasiness, or pain, or jealousy:
We rested in the shade, all pleas'd alike,
Conquer'd and Conqueror (65—)

Wordsworth, in seeking a more truly social development,
comes to realize that what he needs is a just balance between a
wholesome mildness of spirit, or a natural humility, and the
essential energy of rugged individual strength. There are disadvantages in an extreme either way. What he desires is a corrective, but he would risk the danger of an emphasis favoring per-

sonal mildness, if a choice is to be made. This quality of character, however, brings one close to the dangers of introversion. In Wordsworth there developed for a time "a diffidence and modesty" and he

> was taught to feel, perhaps too much,
> The self-sufficing power of solitude. (77—)

The values and the disadvantages of youthful periods of solitude and introversion must be carefully assayed. In this regard Wordsworth was ambivalent in his feelings in youth — and later in college. He found solitude attractive, though he was also strongly drawn to close association with his fellow human beings. Continuing, *The Prelude* gives account of various social experiences of Wordsworth and his young friends which are presented in such a way as to cast upon them a delicate light or coloring of the imagination. Among them there are "rustic dinners on the cool green ground" and the experience of galloping wildly on hired horses to destinations "too distant far" for the time which was available. On one such occasion they reached a sheltered spot where their

> Horses grazed: to more than inland peace
> Left by the sea wind passing overhead ... (115—)

The modifying force of beauty and mood stands in contrast, in this passage, to the violence of boyish energy that the poet portrays in various passages. On one occasion, the youths, having remounted their horses, pursue again their "uncouth race," leaving behind a "single Wren" that Wordsworth would gladly have listened to in mild passiveness. This bird sang "so sweetly in the Nave" that in the "gloom" of the church the developing poet could gladly have made its dark "dwelling-place" his own and "liv'd for ever there"; nevertheless, he says about his group and their boyish activities,

through the Walls we flew
And down the valley, and a circuit made
In wantonness of heart ... (135—)

The time comes, however, when the boy Wordsworth even
more fully appreciates the beauty of the world through
recognizing more particularly values other than those of sheer
physical delight. At this later stage he finds himself seeking
nature for "her own sake," though it is often difficult, he says,
to tell precisely what moments of one's life occasion this. For

who shall parcel out
His intellect, by geometric rules,
Split, like a province, into round and square?
Who knows the individual hour in which
His habits were first sown, even as a seed,
Who that shall point, as with a wand, and say,
'This portion of the river of my mind
Came from yon fountain?' (208—)

Wordsworth feels that Coleridge, being one who is deeply
versed in introspection, will realize the basis for the idea that
the mind cannot be completely explained by a mechanical or
an unimaginative science. By an unimaginative science we
mean separateness: for example, science based, as Whitehead
says, on the "assumption of individually existent physical
bodies, with merely external relationships." [1] That is, we are
referring to the commonly understood inheritance from
Newtonian science. As Wordsworth continues he points out, by
inference, his own view which parallels that of Coleridge who
perceives in a primordial or primary fashion, rather than by
means of a "false secondary power" that is based upon things
— or material objects.

The primordial is connected with the divine here, as it is also
in certain related contexts of Whitehead. The nature of our

limited perception, in Wordsworth's view, is that we are often mistakenly prone to think that the "boundaries," or the *means* by which we perceive, are themselves "things"; these "boundaries" are frequently made by us into what might be called a distinct subsistence, possessing the quality of what appears to many people as an ultimate truth. This is a point which Wordsworth doubly emphasizes when he explains that Coleridge is "unblinded" by such "outward shows"; and hence it is that for anyone, as the poet believes, a greater sense of the "unity of all" may be perceived. Whitehead in his many attacks upon materialism emphasizes a similar need for unity of vision.

Today we have come to know these facts more fully. But there is always a tendency to forget that the "boundaries" which we place upon our thought (for the purpose, it may be, of a particular limited experiment in the field of science) do not represent the actual *thing* as it is in itself. In *The Prelude* it is plain, as we shall soon see, that Wordsworth distinctly realized that scientific knowledge must be understood as relative to that limited frame of relationships within which a particular investigation has been undertaken, and that it is always important to recognize and designate as clearly as we can the limits in the meanings of the terms which are employed. This is not, of course, to deny the importance of the "prop" (as Wordsworth puts it) which scientific investigation may, in innumerable ways, provide for man's activities.

Science, as we know it today, is fundamentally important to the practices of man; its position in this sense is impregnable. But it is essential, too, that man must attempt to sketch out his wider frames of reference. And herein may lie an important part of the use of poetry. The scientist in so far as he speculatively sketches the wider area which surrounds his individual experiment is working in a field which is akin to the poet's. But just as the things which we develop within our minds — for the purpose of enlarging the domain of science — are *constructs*, or things which we "have made," as Words-

51

worth says, so also there arises the problem of the "construct" of the self which comes into being within our consciousness. Wordsworth gives thought to the problem of the "self" — to the question of exactly what one's inner and outer being may consist of. We are placing in quotation marks terms that the poet himself uses because we wish to emphasize the kind of ideas that he definitely has.

The analysis of the nature of personal selfhood is difficult for Wordsworth, or for anyone. Reflection on what Whitehead has said concerning the self can be helpful here in that he makes a case for continuity of the person even in the split-second experiences of the personality, just as he elsewhere stresses the continuity of all things. Whitehead is implicitly acknowledging the difficulty we have in analyzing the self in his comments on "our derivation from our immediate past of a quarter of a second ago." [2] We now are, he goes on to say, in part what we were — that is, "are continuous with" what we were, "the same as it, prolonging its affective tone, enjoying its data." But "we are modifying it, deflecting it, changing its purposes. . . ." And shortly thereafter he adds, "We are different from it, and yet we retain our individual identity with it. This is the mystery of personal identity . . ." Considering such aspects, and Wordsworth's thought also, it becomes evident that it is hard to analyze individual personal identity or personality

> in which,
> Not only general habits and desires,
> But each most obvious and particular thought,
> Not in a mystical and idle sense,
> But in the words of reason deeply weigh'd
> Hath no beginning. (232—)

For Wordsworth the analysis of individual personal identity, touched upon in his passage of *The Prelude*, is a matter requiring profundity of thought, comparable in certain ways to that which Whitehead would require. Whitehead's view of the self also parallels his conception of nature and its passing phenomena which are involved in the creative and in all time. Similarly Wordsworth sees these things as a resultant of time with "no beginning." The word "mystical" in the passage that has been quoted previously is used by the poet in a derogatory sense. Though it is evident, in the whole *Prelude*, that he feels a value in experiences having what might be called a "mystical" tinge, he nevertheless recognizes that confusion of thought may occur if one too loosely and easily follows the beckoning of matters in which imaginative or intuitive powers play a part. Still, the poem makes clear the perception of the fact that even a baby in his mother's arms experiences, in somewhat Gestaltian fashion, the wholeness of things, for it

Is prompt and watchful, eager to combine
In one appearance, all the elements
And parts of the same object, else detach'd
And loth to coalesce. (247—)

The Gestaltian psychologist today would probably not wish to use the word "eager" as it is employed in connection with "to combine" in the first line of this passage, but his idea is nevertheless close to that of Wordsworth here. A being like man, the poet goes on to say, is a "creator and receiver both," and this dual capacity (essentially a combined *imaginative* function) appears even in the earliest stages of human development. Thus Wordsworth presents his ideas of a sort of relatedness, explaining how the "mind spreads" under the influence of "forms which it receives." There is a "Presence" from which a power is brought to us capable of irradiating the "objects" that surround us — the objects that are involved in the "intercourse of sense." Thus our life is characterized by interaction, but we are also "connected with the world." Continuing, Wordsworth (using italics) stresses the "*active* universe" and the fact that we are creators, not merely receivers. This activity-principle Whitehead also well appreciates. The spirit of our life, Wordsworth says, is at times "abated and suppress'd" but it can, in certain possible instances, continue

> Through every change of growth or of decay,
> Pre-eminent till death. (279—)

What might be called "poetic" feeling or poetic sympathy is a quality which is in all cases veritably a part of the life of the individual, Wordsworth feels, and it later may manifest itself in one of the various forms of art; it tends to be almost universally present in the growing child, if circumstances are favorable. It *may* be and often is destroyed, however, in the later stages of childhood. In *The Prelude* Wordsworth has attempted to show how, in his own experience, it was stimulated and "augmented."

But now a trouble came to him, he says, for he was "left alone" to seek his basis in the tangible world. The reference here is to the fact that he had lost his parents. His mother and father had died, the former just before he was eight years old and the latter when he was fourteen. A great deal was lost to him at this stage, the support of his "affections" having vanished although "the building" remained, to all appearances, erect. The structure of the self was sustained, Wordsworth tells us, as if by its own intangible being or spirit. What had occurred before in his development was by no means undone, but now, for a while, he directed his feeling and attention to

> the minuter properties
> Of objects which already were belov'd,
> And of those only. (301—)

Wordsworth had at this stage an interest in separate objects, but it was the particular things in their especial isolation which attracted him and offered a point for focal attention. This type of attention may be good, indeed invaluable. We may remember here the instruction given by the great teacher, Alexander Agassiz (1835-1910), under whom Shaler gained knowledge of attentiveness to fact. The lesson which Shaler learned was the observation of what Wordsworth calls the minuter properties of things. Agassiz gave his pupil Shaler a fish and told him to examine it and then come back and tell what he had noticed about it. After a relatively short while Shaler returned to Agassiz to report what he had discovered. The discoveries he had made, however, were mere commonplaces; he had to learn to look more closely and in the process spent three weeks or more at the task. Wordsworth speaks of natural appearances that are in the world outside us — appearances that have been hitherto unnoticed. The essential feature of scientific observation and its importance appears in this form of attentiveness. The habit of giving very close, even minute attention to material things became a great source of happiness to him at a time of life when what Aristotle regarded as the universal impulse toward the joy in knowledge is particularly enhanced. Such was the period to which Wordsworth pays tribute, "when," as he says, "all knowledge is delight"; in these moments of careful attention during our youth "sorrow is not there."

Great value can be found in such activities of attentiveness as we have described. But also in the process, as Wordsworth experienced it, he felt he was being very strongly drawn, in his emphasis, to transitory things. What he is thinking of in connection with transitoriness is the difficult problem of time, to which Whitehead, partly under the influence of Plato, paid much attention. Our world, in our most casual activities, is *in* time, but there are special perceptions which we may attain, and these perceptions, or insights, can carry us in certain respects beyond the world which is transitory. In the view of Whitehead, the acts of transition themselves carry us forward into something pointing toward the eternal.

For Wordsworth (and for Whitehead) the concentration upon the things of time brings its useful accretion of knowledge in many avenues. But in such a concentratedness, Wordsworth tells us, he had, among other interests, come to enjoy solitude too greatly. At the time he did not realize this, however, for a life in solitude seemed to him "more active" than that of living social intercourse even at its best. Here we see the notion, sometimes expressed in our own day, that the highest kind of inner activity of man must, for the most part, be pursued on an individual basis. The individualistic argument may attempt to oppose the democratic ideal on the ground that there are various dangers before a person in that he may wrongly grade himself and certain others down, and thus underestimate what he and other special persons are capable of, and what they should *do*. Thus it is, that we may often underestimate the real and important powers of human beings to make significant contributions. If one assumes this attitude he tends to shy away from any action which might be understood by his fellows as pseudo-aristocratic.

The value, on the other hand, of working alone — even "aristocratically" — expresses itself for the moment in Wordsworth in the new fashion in which he came to perceive "manifold distinctions" in which "the common eye" observes no differences. In his solitary walks he had formed the practice of being attentive to the multitude of sounds which he could distinguish. To this habit his poetry bears eloquent record. Something of the modern psychological theory concerning a collective unconsciousness may be suggested in Wordsworth's statement

> I would stand,
> Beneath some rock, listening to sounds that are
> The ghostly language of the ancient earth,
> Or make their dim abode in distant winds.

Thence did I drink the visionary power.
I deem not profitless these fleeting moods
Of shadowy exultation . . . (326—)

It was from experiences like these, then, that he drank "visionary power." Indeed, the sounds he refers to "are kindred to our purer mind" — they are connected with the human "intellectual life"; more than this, they contribute to a subtle "sense" related to "sublimity," and this sense, Wordsworth says, leads to the recognition of the infinite. Again we use quotation marks around certain words to emphasize the definite presence of specific ideas in Wordsworth. The contribution of a subtle sense related to the sublime and to infinity occurs through the action of our tendency to

aspire
With faculties still growing, feeling still
That whatsoever point they gain, they still
Have something to pursue. (338—)

Wordsworth's conceptions with regard to the sublime — and the relation the sublime has to the tendency of the individual to aspire — appear frequently in a circumstance in which he is situated in solitude. These conceptions occur, for example, in his observation of storms or when he is above what he calls the "mundane world." Despite his great appreciation of ordinary people, he does not overlook the fact that there are experiences, even in childhood or youth, which one may have that are above the casual events in the lives of those who are mundane, or to use another of his own images, those who are dwellers in the valleys. Such conceptions came to him, he says, not merely in his observations of "grandeur" but also when he observed "tranquil scenes"; they arise, he believes, from

that universal power

And fitness in the latent qualities
And essences of things, by which the mind
Is mov'd by feelings of delight . . . (343—)

Often Wordsworth arose very early in the morning to go on walks, or, after his wanderings, he sat "among the hills" on an out-jutting rock in a moment in which the whole world seemed to be in "utter solitude." Such experiences, as conceived by the poet, were evidently not simply aesthetic. They brought with them "a holy calm" giving rise to a state in which he seemed to have no "bodily eyes"; what he saw seemed like something within the self, somewhere between appearance and reality. When we consider the problem of appearance and reality, we are again on the borderline of the great philosophical problem of time, or the question that Whitehead refers to as the *passage* which is within nature. "There is the deep underlying Harmony of Nature, as it were a fluid flexible support; and on its surface the ripples of social efforts, harmonizing and clashing in their aims at ways of satisfaction." [3] This statement is drawn from Whitehead's penetrating chapter on "Peace," which is concerned with a calmness of the self. Wordsworth's "holy calm" which brought with it a state in which he seemed to have no "bodily eyes" affected him in such a way that the things he saw appeared like something in himself, "a dream" — a force almost within his consciousness only. Thus it was that in a "spirit of religious love" he finally "walked with nature." He possessed now, as seemed clearly evident, the initiating power of creativity, despite his seeming passiveness — though, for the most part, his spirit was, in this period

Subservient strictly to external things
With which it commun'd. (386—)

Surprisingly, in spite of the progress in a new direction that Wordsworth had been making, we still find, it seems, an overstress upon "external things" that remains within his nature. He can be even "subservient" to a material world. In effect this means he was more or less unconsciously trying to hold fast to what we might today call a reality principle: he is even leaning a bit backwards as he is striving to retain the balance of qualities necessary to an adequate vision of the world. Wordsworth recognizes that the spiritual is important in life. But he believes that it is possible to see the spiritual in the natural, and thus to find his way through his problems which take him into difficult processes of thought. Apart from Wordsworth's subservience to "external things" there remained the "auxiliar light" coming from within the self which even

> on the setting sun
> Bestow'd new splendor . . . (386—)

For Wordsworth the very "midnight storm" was held to be influenced by his actively functioning subjectivity. As he tells us, it darkened increasingly under the effect produced by his "eye." Such a function of the subjective principle within the self was a labor which was essentially "pleasing" to him. Following his treatment of this theme he goes on to tell of his "observation of affinities" which are not observed by "common minds." Again at this point we may feel troubled by an apparent slight being given to the commonality of human beings — in a word, the overly individualistic tendency of the poet, or the seeming devotion to a pseudo-aristocratic principle.

But Wordsworth, in his reference to the "observation of affinities" which are not commonly seen, wishes rather to emphasize the need of a sense of intellectual adventure whereby one is willing to compare things which in the view of some persons are regarded as incapable of bearing comparison. The "affinities" in things not commonly seen which Wordsworth mentions may bring to mind novel or unconventional relationships that Whitehead refers to, an example of which appears in his somewhat bald statement: "A game of football is perhaps a faint reflection of the Battle of Marathon." [4] In the context he goes on to suggest that experience "in all ages and circumstances has common qualities." But there are, however, much more extreme comparisons which Whitehead makes. Like Wordsworth, he is able to perceive radical affinities between things which to most people would seem far afield.

Wordsworth speaks of unusual affinities as we have seen; for him radical affinities exist between objects which to the majority of persons, perhaps contain no reasonable kinship. A better analogy than the relationship of Marathon to a football match appears in Whitehead's references to number in which, in reflecting on two groups, we may be "thinking of those relationships between those two groups which are entirely independent of the individual essences of any of the members of either group." [5] Conceivably under certain circumstances we could add together geese, horses, motor cars, fishes, and days. Such an action would be "a very remarkable feat of abstraction. . . ." The correspondences of things that Wordsworth carried in his mind also, then, were not simple; they were not the obvious one-to-one relationships that thousands of people —unimaginative because of their training — find alone permissible. As he says,

> To unorganic natures I transferr'd
> My own enjoyments . . . (410—)

The effect of his experiences served to unify his personality in such fashion that all his thoughts "were steep'd in feeling," and, under the influence of a profound associationism, all his feelings were interpenetrated with thought. The value of such a result, stressed frequently in twentieth-century critical thinking, is to a certain extent an outgrowth of the influence of the English romantic movement upon us, though it is generally related to the influence of the poet John Donne. In Wordsworth

it is only a portion of his feeling of the total unity — or of that
being which is

> spread
> O'er all that moves, and all that seemeth still,
> O'er all, that, lost beyond the reach of thought
> And human knowledge, to the human eye
> Invisible, yet liveth to the heart,
> O'er all that leaps, and runs, and shouts, and sings,
> Or beats the gladsome air, o'er all that glides
> Beneath the wave, yea in the wave itself
> And mighty depths of waters. (420—)

This passage may be connected with the earlier associational
passage in "Tintern Abbey" where Wordsworth stresses the
unity of being. In *The Prelude* passage, however, he goes on to
declare that "in all things" he "saw one life;" this reference to
seeing one life in all things brings Wordsworth a still greater
recognition of the integration within himself, which in turn
leads to feelings of security, and, ultimately, to a sense of
almost complete well-being or joy. He feels that he has been
communing both with nature and God, the former — nature —
being a force which may be metaphorically conceived as a living thing. Indeed, it *is* a living thing, Wordsworth believes —
itself a work of God in which man may come close to perceiv-
ing the creator in his handiwork.

Here we must be aware of the dangers in the misapplication
of the conception of pantheism to the poet's point of view.
What is crucial as to this may be made somewhat more clear if
we recall Whitehead's comment on "the history of Western
thought"; this history, he says, may be seen as consisting "in
the attempted fusion" [6] of the doctrine of law in the universe as
imposed by command (which so often finds exemplification in
primitive religions) and law as a thing of *immanence*. In the
ultimately *polarized* attitudes "of the two doctrines of Law" we

are led "on the one hand to the extreme monotheistic doctrine of God, as essentially transcendent and only accidentally immanent, and on the other hand to the pantheistic doctrine. . . ." But the history of human thought leads in general to neither extreme, and in this the Greeks point the way — so Whitehead holds. The preferred approach, he believes, is that of Plato, not that of pantheism. Wordsworth, we may conclude, is in the tradition stemming from Plato, a tradition which moves on in the twentieth century to thinkers like Whitehead. Explaining briefly his conception of God, Whitehead writes elsewhere: "The notion of God . . . is that of an actual entity immanent in the actual world, but transcending any finite cosmic event — a being at once actual, eternal, immanent, and transcendent." [7]

Wordsworth has dealt thus far in *The Prelude* mainly with nature, which, being immediately present to man and being influential upon him in his most rudimentary development, tends to serve, broadly speaking, as the first focal center of one's thought. This emphasis continues until such a time as a person begins to understand more fully his own psychological make-up and his own personal function — in a word, his own place in the world. Along with the theme of nature the author has been treating a kind of visionary theme. Wordsworth was aware that sneers, as he says, may perhaps be directed toward this latter interest but his goal, if he can reach it, is an important one. What he is mainly driving toward, we may say, is an inquiry such as Whitehead later made into the possible grounds for faith in life and in humanity.

The point of initial departure that Whitehead used, for his purposes, was science. Now, in anticipation of our next chapter, which concerns Wordsworth's experience of education at the University of Cambridge, we may mention a matter connected with the poet's earlier school days which has a bearing on science. Neither Wordsworth nor Whitehead focuses philosophy in a major way upon science, but it was for each of them a point of departure. From Wordsworth's biography we learn that he had been brought in contact with unusual standards of education even in his pre-university school days. At this point of preparatory training he was under the influence of his teacher, William Taylor, who himself had been distinguished, we are told, for his "extensive learning" [8] and who had been a fellow at Cambridge University before he took up his duties as a schoolmaster.

While under Taylor's influence, in 1785, Wordsworth had written a poem for the local school's bicentenary in which the Spirit of Education speaks, emphasizing the importance of science and the contribution to human thought of Sir Francis Bacon's method and its relation to nature. Taylor was probably a stimulus to the poet not only in this respect, however, but in keen perceptiveness in connection with poetry. Students today would be fortunate if at an early stage they could enjoy close personal contact with a man of Taylor's ability. Still, the major drift of Wordsworth's life — including a kind of expansiveness — takes him beyond science and the general point of view of this teacher, as we shall see in the next chapter.

### Footnotes

1. *Process and Reality*, p. 471.
2. *Adventures of Ideas*, p. 269. See also his remarks (p. 235) concerning the "direct observation of the past with the intention of finding its completion in the present fact."
3. *Ibid.*, p. 369.
4. *The Aims of Education and Other Essays*, Third Printing (New York: Macmillan Co., 1966), p. 101.
5. *Science and the Modern World*, p. 30.
6. *Adventures of Ideas*, p. 154.
7 *Process and Reality* (New York: Macmillan, 1929, 1960), p. 143.
8. Mary Moorman, *William Wordsworth — A Biography: The Early Years* (Oxford, 1957), p. 50. The words quoted are George Dyer's.

## Chapter III

# Wordsworth's First Residence at Cambridge Re-examined in Relation to Whitehead's Thought

Near the close of the last chapter we spoke of faith in life and in humanity. We may ask, now, does an experience of a student in a university — for Wordsworth refers in Book Three of *The Prelude* to his experience of this kind — contribute to such a faith? Is it *likely* to do so? Does it provide the long view? Here we may consider for a moment a suggestion of current importance to us in Whitehead's works though he is offering it in a context referring to the development of an early university — in ancient Alexandria, as it happens. "It is no wonder," Whitehead remarks, "that the first emergence of modern scholarship studied in a modern university, took place when

64

Platonic speculation was transferred to a land of old professional activity." [1] He is thinking here of both philosophy and technology. The situation in universities today is, he believes, somewhat similar to the Alexandrian situation in that our professions, technological and otherwise, have played an important part generally in the development of our modern higher education.

But it is the *speculative* side of universities, as we might expect, not the professional side, that Whitehead in the context we have referred to values most. And it is here — in considering the speculative — that the problem of a certain measure of confidence in life becomes a factor of importance. It is important, Whitehead feels, because speculation "obtains its urge from a deep ultimate faith, that through and through the nature of things is penetrable by reason." Universities contribute a kind of confidence. Here is an extremely vital side of the university spirit — faith in the world — as will become more clearly evident. But Whitehead makes a further point of significance. Scholarship is characteristic of universities, and scholarship in a sense places its emphasis on tradition. It very gradually builds up modes of approach to problems, and it tends to preserve through time "accepted methodologies"; in this respect it is beneficently "conservative of belief." Here, however, we are looking upon the surface of the university. There is also another point subtly implied. Underneath all, a university's "tone of mind leads toward a fundamental negation."

The view of a university we have presented, with its characteristic negation, or its skepticism which is implied here, is, Whitehead thinks, in the main sound. Skepticism is prominent. A university has to be characterized by much head-shaking and many doubts. But however we may judge this interpretation of the university spirit, there is the further matter of the relation between Whitehead's educational conceptions and those of Wordsworth. In the poet's thought there are many doubts, and there is the problem of law and impulse. He fluc-

tuates in his thought in regard to the university, ideal or otherwise.

Wordsworth has a feeling for law, but like many poets he is
prone to impulse — this is true especially in his youth. But he
comes more and more to recognize the importance of a
philosophy based on an overall *law*. Let us emphasize the
points we have been making by the following statement, this
time drawn from Whitehead: "The notion of Law, that is to
say, of some measure of regularity or of persistence or recurrence, is an essential element in the urge toward technology,
methodology, scholarship, and speculation." [2] All of the last
three factors — methodology, scholarship, and speculation —
are of great importance in Whitehead's idea of a university,
though for him there are, of course, other forces in the university spirit.

We have seen in what has been said thus far a kind of ten-
sion between three of the forces that, for Whitehead, are
characteristically at work in a university: law (or regularity),
negation, and speculativeness. All three of these forces were important to the nature of philosophy, for Whitehead and Wordsworth. Furthermore, all three forces have a place in the poet's
experience at the University of Cambridge. Regularity (even
rigor) had no small place in Wordsworth's theory of education,
though, as a youth, he had his full share of rebellion of spirit
against being over-controlled. But, more — he was from an early stage a developing writer, a creative person. And who can
doubt that he would give his assent to the importance of the in-
citing, the impelling force of imagination in the ideal educational program? This is a point in education strongly stressed
by Whitehead; thus he begins a paragraph emphatically, "The
justification for a university is that it preserves the connection
between knowledge and the zest of life, by uniting the young
and the old in the imaginative consideration of learning. The
university imparts information, but it imparts it
imaginatively." [3] This it should do. And he adds a moment

later: "A university which fails in this respect has no reason for existence."

Universities — in their complex character and in their connection with life — have at times been compared to cities. Even in the Cambridge of Wordsworth's day there was a relationship of this kind which is brought out in the poet's experience. And his philosophy is experiential: a matter which is existential. The theme which he presents in Book Three of *The Prelude*, concerns what for him was a comparatively *crowded* world of university life. Cambridge, notwithstanding its lighter, vainer side, acted upon the poet as a cosmic force. It was dynamic and alive. Even from the first autumn day, as he and his fellows approached the region, the place, he says

> seem'd more and more
> To have an eddy's force, and suck'd us in
> More eagerly at every step we took. (10—)

The force Wordsworth felt at this point was doubtless mainly within himself, but for him the University of Cambridge was also in itself a formidable thing. The poet, however, next moves by design from the lofty to the trivial. A philosophy needs its comic corrective. To Wordsworth, the inexperienced novice, the last stages of his ride to the city of new adventure had been momentous as his coach passed "beneath the Castle," and then down to the river, and crossed the river thereafter by way of Magdalene Bridge. In thinking of these things he brings a memorable sentence of description *ironically* to a close with a reference to the "famous Inn" known as "the Hoop," where he finally alighted. There is a cluster of associations here, including perhaps images of childhood and even hoop-rolling: he is presenting what he saw with a kind of dual perception, a double vision. He is capable both of laughing at himself and of being deeply serious. Boylike, he found here and there at the university "acquaintances" in the exciting circumstances, and these youths were quickly glorified in his mind as "friends." His vanity and hero-worship at the time come also into play. He observes with somewhat mixed feelings these

> poor simple Schoolboys, now hung round
> With honour and importance . . . (18—)

Can we notice any connection between philosophy and the things that were happening to Wordsworth in his university days? A person's philosophy is affected by his experience, and the record of that experience can help us to understand better his later, mature thought. Being highly imaginative, Wordsworth, as we might expect, was capable at times of phantasying his experience. Here we use a word which he himself on occasion will employ — he is given to the phantasmal in various forms, or perhaps he creates in his own mind appearances which need adjustment to reality. The world of the poet's university days was, indeed, in many respects a world of seeming which met in idleness as he roamed the streets and quadrangles of his environment. Among these boys, the young Wordsworth went about the matter of settling somewhat pompously to his new life. He paints the picture vividly, and without shame:

> to myself I seem'd
> A man of business and expense, and went
> From shop to shop about my own affairs,
> To Tutors or to Tailors, as befel . . . (23—)

From place to place he wandered "with loose and careless heart." There follow "invitations, suppers, wine, and fruit"; it is all very human. And we must not overlook the fact that in seeking to understand the philosophy of a person, common or homely features of his life may have a place. In contrast to the presentation of the vanity, the self-importance that one feels in youth in a university, *The Prelude* gives us undertones of serious things — an example of which for Wordsworth was the venerable association-filled college, St. John's, which he was now entering. The reference he makes to the most mystical of those figures to whom authorship of the gospels is attributed raises the tone of *The Prelude* to a height of profound seriousness. There is something of mystery in the following lines which probably contain for Wordsworth a measure of symbolism —

> The Evangelist St. John my Patron was,
> Three gloomy Courts are his; and in the first
> Was my abiding place . . . (44—)

This symbolism of darkness and mystery may be perceived here despite the fact that the lines are soon followed by a descent in tone in the reference to the poet's "abiding-place" as an "obscure" nook. The contrast is striking. Beneath his room, furthermore, he hears throughout the term the college kitchen making a not altogether pleasant "humming sound, less tuneable than bees," evidence of the industrious workers below. Along with this murmuring sound, there is a mixture of shouts of "sharp command and scolding"; in addition to this there was the chime of the clock in Trinity's towers never ceasing its quarterly reminder, night and day, of the inexorable passage of time. A sense of sound is emphasized here, giving the reader a feeling of the weight of what Whitehead calls *passage*, which includes mortality. Apart from the aural appeal which the poet makes use of there is of course the visual aspect of the setting. From his bedroom he could see "a few yards off" the building which contained the statue of the illustrious graduate, Sir Isaac Newton, "with his Prism and silent Face."

When we think of Newton in this context, the idea of studying in the Cambridge setting might well seem inspiring. But there were certain elements of detraction. Wordsworth indicates a fundamental objection to the competitive spirit of examinations, with their trembling hopes and "small jealousies"; these were not for him. Combat in study (as he conceives the competitive program) had small attraction. He tells us that he sought little in the way of "honors" and it is not surprising that he won little in such enterprise.

This is perhaps a subject about which he was sensitive, for he returns to it later. In his old age, also, he reported on competition in studies, indicating that the jealousy and envy in such competition were sickening to him in his youth. Now — at the time represented in *The Prelude* — rather than engage in such a contest he tells us that he preferred to refrain from having any part in the struggle. Connected with such emotions, it seems, was the further fact that his mind often held "melancholy thoughts" concerning his family as well as "some fears" about his future. But Wordsworth realized that, whatever its disadvantages, his present situation was fortunate. He was coming now to recognize somewhat more fully the powers that were his and to appreciate the fact that his experience at Cambridge would bring newly extended opportunities for spreading his thoughts toward wider horizons.

Aside from the direct relationships connected with university life which Wordsworth had, he continued to spend such time as he could in the open country. In his appreciation of "rock, fruit, or flower" he projected something of himself into the objects. As he tells us, he actually perceived them feel, or, in his words, at times "saw them feel"; in other respects he simply "link'd them to some feeling," and, as they became part of what he calls a "mass," they entered his very personality and finally "respired with inward meaning." It is at first sight a strange conception that he presents. But the inward self is active, as it is in Whitehead's thought, and the whole philosophy the poet attains is analogous to that of the philosopher and no less startling as it grows upon the reader. Here we can see that by actual belief, or by analogy, Wordsworth animated the universe as he had done earlier in the Lake Country — perhaps, within his mind, doing so even more completely now. This animation of things in the universe might seem superficial, but Wordsworth's thought here has some connection with certain ideas of our own century. In the unity of Whitehead's philosophy, for example, complexities of feeling have an important place.

Things for Whitehead also, then, in a sense feel, and in addition they are linked to some feeling. Like Wordsworth, he descends "the scale of organic being" — Whitehead puts the matter in this way — and he says that "animals, and even vegetables, in low forms of organism exhibit modes of behavior directed towards self-preservation. There is every indication," he says, "of a vague feeling of causal relationship with the external world, of some intensity, vaguely defined as to quality . . ." In the same context Whitehead explains his own position by saying that his "philosophy of organism attributes 'feeling' throughout the actual world." [4] What he says here, however, has a connection with his critical ideas about pantheism which we presented near the close of the preceding chapter where we referred to immanence and transcendence. The view that he personally holds is not pantheistic but one including transcendence.

In our present discussion we have seen Wordsworth referring to "rock, fruit, or flower" and projecting something of himself into them; he "saw them feel" or connected them to "some feeling" in himself. What this actually brought him was an increased sensitivity to the unity in all things — a sense, that is, of "the one Presence" and of the fact that there is a "Life" within "the great whole" which is an animating force. This experience to Wordsworth contains something larger than immanence and transcendence as the terms are usually understood. That is, immanence may be mistakenly thought of in such a way that it is carried to the uttermost extreme, and

71

transcendence, in contrast, may at times also be magnified to the point of grandiloquence. The poet is avoiding either extreme. As he continues, he says that he was now "most rich." He "had a world" which surrounded him and which he possessed: he had "made it; for it only liv'd" within himself and in addition it existed "to the God who look'd" inwardly upon his (the poet's) own "mind." He declares that this "was no madness," though it might appear to be so.

How does he justify the rationality of this force? He "had an eye" of power, he says, operating in his "strongest workings" and this eye

> Was looking for the shades of difference
> As they lie hid in all exterior forms,
> Near or remote, minute or vast, an eye
> Which from a stone, a tree, a wither'd leaf,
> To the broad ocean and the azure heavens,
> Spangled with kindred multitudes of stars
> Could find no surface where its power might sleep . . .
> (158—)

These things — a stone, a tree, a leaf — Wordsworth tells us he closely observed. He noted that no two forms are ever the same; everywhere is difference, uniqueness, individuality. We find the same point in Whitehead — "nothing ever recurs in exact detail." [5] For Wordsworth — and for Whitehead — all, nevertheless, is one. The poet goes on to assert that this is a subject fit for an epic, though it involves the interior history of the mind where it must be sensed faintly, imperfectly "far hidden from the reach of words." His poetry illustrates here the tendency of the literature of romanticism to move toward expansiveness to which we have earlier referred. The poet is centering consciously, as we see, upon that which he feels is *inexpressible* and virtually infinite. "Human life," as Whitehead also says, "is driven forward by its dim apprehension of notions too general for its existing language." [6] Wordsworth likewise is concerned with human life and the individual personality — itself, as the poet believes, connected with the infinite. But there is also a loneliness within the self and this is important. In *The Prelude* he indicates

> Points have we all of us within our souls,
> Where all stand single . . . (186—)

Wordsworth is struck by the fact that the human being has "incommunicable powers." At the same time he stresses the fact that each person in his psychological nature becomes a memory — he becomes "a memory to himself." The peculiar separate consciousness of the individual, the separateness of the self referred to by Wordsworth, is a point brought out also in an essay by Wheelock. This essay is of interest because of its relation not only to Wordsworth's thought but to that of Whitehead. In it Wheelock quotes a statement to the effect that poetry is a "form of language that tries to say the unsayable" [7]; in his discussion of this idea he considers the paradox of the separate self and the peculiar character of poetry.

The special nature of poetry, as Wheelock says, "is not communication as we ordinarily understand it." Our problem, therefore, is to bridge the gap, as he remarks a little earlier in the page from which we have quoted. What he says in the preceding page is also important. We must bridge the gap so that words may truly be "symbols of the unity existing throughout the parts of one multitudinous Self"; the idea here, including the conception of the multitudinous character of one's personal being, has analogies to a conception in Whitehead's philosophy, and the essay by Wheelock is of decided value to anyone who is trying to understand the philosopher's thinking. It is in the direction of such thought that Wordsworth too, proceeds. The pertinence of the poet's philosophy to the modern situation may be recognized in the concept which

73

Wheelock applies to our own time.

Everything that we have said concerning Wordsworth is related not only to the few among men but — broadly speaking — to all of us — for, as the poet believes, "we" possess "majestic sway," by natural means, in the very "strength of nature." The word "we" includes all of us. A feeling much the same as Wordsworth's here — and elsewhere in *The Prelude* — is implied in Wheelock's essay. The essay also is connected with Martin Buber, as we would expect. The "separation into selves" in our human life, Wheelock says, "makes communication necessary," but "it is their basic oneness that makes it possible." [8] There is a great twentieth-century need, as we may all admit, for a poetry that could reach mankind generally. This need is based on the idea that communication itself "predicates a prior mutual agreement resting upon the correspondences between selves that, though separate, at root are one."

Here Wheelock, like Wordsworth, hopes for a more complete rapport among mankind, an advance of "the social and co-operative virtues" over the "aggressive and competitive instincts," which he says are less essential in a world of crowded existence than they were at a time in which opportunity for all was more open and available — for example in early America. England in Wordsworth's day, however — unlike America — did not have a readily available frontier waiting to be preempted, and this may account in part for the presence of Wordsworth's strong emphasis upon the social and co-operative virtues.

As we have seen, the limitations of the aggressive and competitive instincts were apparent to Wordsworth even when he was a university student and earlier. Connected with this is his attitude toward liberalism. The atmosphere at Cambridge was somewhat liberal, as he suggests. The influence of republican thought, then current in France, may well have been a factor here. But Wordsworth does not present the picture of Cambridge as that of an ideal university, in its political features or in any other way. His sight, though at first "dazzled by the novel show" of a new experience, did not remain long misled by any of the glitter around him. He repeatedly returned to himself, despite momentary self-disloyalties. So he speaks about his disloyalties, in a spirit of self-criticism. But though a life of "empty noise" often succeeded his moments of more profound insight into things, he did not let such raucousness overwhelm him. He was, of course, subject to that common failing of youth, irresolution. He is honest in his admission of

> a treasonable growth
> Of indecisive judgments that impair'd
> And shook the mind's simplicity. (214—)

With all the drawbacks of his youth and his circumstances, however, Wordsworth made a reckoning of himself and his shortcomings, and he was moved thereafter to express an appreciation of what Cambridge had offered him. It was a fortunate time in his life to be in so great a place, he says, surrounded by "so many happy Youths," in a "budding-time" — with "health, and hope, and beauty" in a place "famous through the world"; the experience was, for him, indeed a "goodly" one. During this period of university life, Wordsworth experienced, too, further semi-mystical moments — periods when spells descended on him. But despite his momentary moods of aloofness, which contributed to what was almost a meditativeness of a spiritual sort, he was basically gregarious and if he found himself in a crowd he was drawn to it, for he says his

> heart
> Was social, and lov'd idleness and joy. (235—)

In the face of this gregariousness which — it is true — contributed to his widening capacity for human understanding, he had a dim sense of passing from "the remembrances of better things"; he felt that his spirit had in some ways become tarnished. Nevertheless in this "first act" of university experience, he says, he could not step on the very ground "where the grass had yielded to the steps" that certain others had made, without from time to time feeling deeply moved. These others represented complete "generations of illustrious Men" and could well be considered in a spirit of veneration. Here he was passing from one place to another "by the same Gateways," sleeping "where they had slept," meeting the dawn as they had done, and ranging the same "enclosure old" — this he could not do "undisturb'd."

The image that comes to his mind as he thinks of his brilliant predecessors contains a darkness associated with grandeur: his "illustrious" forerunners are set in Rembrandtian fashion against shadows. Yet paradoxically these same men seemed close to him also. When he pictured them in his mind, as they were when young — perhaps callow — they seemed veritably to be like his own compatriots. Earlier he had referred to Newton with great awe. Now he says,

> Place also by the side of this dark sense
> Of nobler feeling, that those spiritual Men,
> Even the great Newton's own etherial Self,
> Seem'd humbled in these precincts . . . (268—)

Thus although there was an atmosphere of greatness clinging about the university for him, this very greatness contributed to the poet's sense of the commonalty of men. Should we view great human beings with an awe that is stultifying to others who up to the present have achieved less? Are we wise to stress in our minds possible achievements that various individuals can work *toward*? All along Wordsworth is thinking of the hopes that may be in the hearts of human beings, driving them

76

on to aspiring efforts. As he thinks of those who have been great in the past — and their actions at the college stage — he concludes that such young persons while at Cambridge also had to perform their lowly intellectual duties; they were "invested" with these "tasks," and were not too exalted to wear the cloak of the most "plain business" of life, day after day.

We have had to paraphrase many passages of *The Prelude* in order to blend the poet's materials together for the purpose of this book, and we shall often have to paraphrase further in the pages that follow. The purpose of this procedure has been covered in our "Introduction." But now we can pause for a moment to consider Wordsworth's situation at the stage we have reached. Possibly he could have gained more in his first year at Cambridge if the system there had followed what Whitehead has termed a vital "Rhythm of Education," [9] including a stage of early stimulus, a later period in which precision is essential, and, finally, a third development of generalization. This may sound technical but here we are talking in terms of an ideal, or an as-if. An as-if is an ideal which is not an altogether perfect reality. It is not a perfect concept. In the view of Whitehead, the cyclical process should be pervasive in education; it should occur and reoccur not only as one is learning new subjects but as one encounters new aspects of subjects. If precision or drudgery is demanded in a multiplicity of things, and at *all* stages of one's encounter with problems, the result is stultifying. If precision or discipline is not developed at the time that it is needed the person who is being educated will have little knowledge of what in the end he may become, and little respect for the process he is undergoing.

Lack of respect in education breeds negligence. Newton too, according to Wordsworth, had to learn respect for this process of human development. There is ideal value in thinking of human beings on a common level. To do so is to apply tentatively a philosophy that has some points of kinship with that of Hans Vaihinger (1852-1933), whose thought had a relationship to the ideas we are here presenting. What this application of a point in philosophy amounts to is that an ideal, though imperfectly conceived or inadequately worked out, may still have a value. Our common life is full of such ideals, which we apply as if they were more perfect than they are. They are thus applied because they have working value. And so it can be with the ideal we perceive when we think of the commonalty of human beings who, because of force of circumstances, or an environment favorable to them, have in the end made astonishing achievements. We can share aspiringly a great deal with such persons.

But to return to Wordsworth's experience at Cambridge, and "life's plain business" as it refers to those who later became illustrious: through this very fact of their more or less humble activity they are the more endearing to us, and they are the more deserving of our veneration and love. Enduring life's routine or wearing that routine as a "daily garb" has its place for everyone. Here it is necessary to speak also about imagination, recalling the reference to it in the early part of this chapter. In Whitehead's view, "the way in which a university should function in the preparation for an intellectual career" involves the promotion of "the imaginative consideration of the various underlying principles"; this is important. "The routine then receives its meaning, and also illuminates the principles which give it that meaning." [10]

The importance of the "drudgery" or discipline of routine, as Whitehead conceives it, needs to be remembered, but drudgery as such should not be given exaggerated emphasis. It does, however, have a relation to the common things of life to which Wordsworth pays respect. The "homely" things of ordinary experience have their place even for those who become very great: thus commonalty is again exemplified by the poet in *The Prelude*. The famous figures who preceded him are conceived in an attractively human way. In his imagination he hears the voice of Chaucer with its laughter of friendliness, and, more loftily, he observes as a brother the silent Spenser

> moving through his clouded heaven
> With the moon's beauty and the moon's soft pace ...
> (281—)

Wordsworth in imagination also watches the singularly youthful Milton "bounding" before him on a Cambridge path among the surrounding "crown" of young men. Many of those who were to become great were not only at Cambridge in the past, but some too may be conceived in their budding time as being present in any generation. They are part of our common humanity. When Wordsworth sets foot in the rooms where the "temperate" Milton passed his Cambridge days, he indulges himself in wine, and is so carried away in the "festive ring" of students that his senses reel. We can sympathize with his feelings: this was no ordinary occasion. The moment, we may observe, leads to his belated rush to chapel, hurrying past "honest burghers," with his student gown upshouldered

> in a dislocated hump
> With shallow ostentatious carelessness ... (316—)

The portrayal of the young Wordsworth here reveals to us that he was capable of being a poseur in his ostentation. Though he was a "democrat," he was not at times above being something of a snob. But his friend, Coleridge, will, he hopes, "forgive the weakness of that hour," with its "unworthy vanities"; indeed, so conscious is Wordsworth of this defection that he says if he were in a confessional mood he would have to admit to a very large number of similar faults.

The poet's dominant remembrance of his first year at Cambridge, however, was of his sloth. The priceless experience of being at a great university was unfortunately undergone in a kind of muddled state of "loose indifference"; he found

79

himself led to uncritical "likings" and remembered woefully his approaches to things at a "low pitch," with "duty" being very remote from his perception. He lacked "rigorous discipline." Indeed, in continuing he confesses:

> Nor was this the blame
> Of others but my own . . . (354—)

Many of us today, looking back upon our education, would admit a sense of guilt such as Wordsworth has expressed in this statement. Certainly if education is in a bad way (as we believe) the fault is in the student almost as much as in the system. Yet the institution usually receives the major criticism from the voice of youth and from others. And so it was with Wordsworth. He fluctuates, like a modern youth, between self-accusation and outward hostility in feelings — and the latter reaction tends perhaps to dominate. It should not be surprising to us, then, that Wordsworth, because of youthful emotions, or remembrances, directs considerable criticism toward the educational establishment. What ought we to blame most when we philosophize, the faults of the individual or those of the environment? In *The Prelude* Wordsworth takes pleasure in contemplating a more nearly ideal university than he has known, to which homage such as he has paid earlier to nature could be "frankly offered up." The basic feature of this dream-university would consist, he says, in its general tone or "temper"; in such an institution aspiration would be important. The "unripe years" of its students

> should be made
> To minister to works of high attempt . . . (393—)

Wordsworth continues the development of his reactions to education by explaining that such an orientation toward learning as he favors would be in the very best sense spiritual, or even "religious"; Whitehead similarly stresses a religious ideal in relation to any education. But in the poet we find a somewhat more extreme statement of the position we are referring to here. There can be, and there should in actuality be, a "holy joy" in learning. By his reference to the "holy" he does not mean anything like a sanctimonious religiosity. This is made clear soon. Wordsworth is emphasizing the idea of a university somewhat in the manner of Newman later; that is, he stresses the importance in higher learning of the pursuit of knowledge, as he puts it, "for its own sake."

The pursuit of knowledge for the sake of knowledge has often been criticized in our day. Whitehead, for example, to a certain extent criticizes it. The ivory tower has at times been taken as an aristocratic ideal to be set in opposition to an education for democracy which is associated with technology and science. But Wordsworth, too, though he refers to the pursuit of knowledge for its own sake, is seeking democracy. He speaks of the importance in education of an openness or simplicity of approach. Here what he seems to have in mind is a complete and unafraid candor — presumably between student and student, or between student and instructor. This spirit he refers to as "republican" in character. Authority, authoritarianism, what Wordsworth might call the monarchism of culture with its "seeming" — or its false-front — he despises.

But if an institution of learning is to have a false front (as so many such institutions do have) let it at any rate, Wordsworth implores, keep itself free from empty religious pretense, with its superficial formulary of forced chapel attendance and idle lip-service. Such a condition, as we know, was prevalent in many American institutions of higher learning even in the early stages of our own century, and Wordsworth's criticism could be directed justifiably to us to some degree at the present time. In his context, drawing upon his personal background in Cumberland and Westmoreland, he thinks of sheep-tending and the wholesome common-sense of the peasant. A peasant would not coerce sheep unduly toward a drinking trough. In this recognition of the value of common-sense Wordsworth asks

> Was ever known
> The witless Shepherd who would drive his Flock
> With serious repetition to a pool
> Of which 'tis plain to sight they never taste? (415—)

Nor does Wordsworth stop with a mere assault upon these clergymen who arbitrarily ruled their college chapels. The university administration is itself assailed. He makes a direct appeal to "presidents" and "Deans" (he capitalizes the title) to put an end to mockery. His satire is biting. Students who attend so-called religious colleges are, he feels, so muddled that when they return to their homes they often carry with them no more than the habit — the facade — of religion. They fail to perceive what, in deeply genuine values for the people, a profound religion could really mean. Hence he says that throughout the country worship even in the remotest hamlets suffers and becomes vitiated. At times the basic superficiality manifested in religiosity may so pervade a university that even science "is smitten" and "loses her just authority"; thus it is that both a superficial science and a trivial religion fall

> beneath
> Collateral suspicion, else unknown. (431—)

Wordsworth believes that a splendid university for the future could be *created*, could receive vital organization. In such a virtual reorganization the university would not be "indigent of songs" — of poetry — or of other creative production. In the past, in certain ages, higher learning has harmonized well with the careers of artists, and he regrets that this is not true of the university of his experience. Here we can think of our own time. In our day, creativity is, of course, beginning to receive decided emphasis. We see it in the university — at Stanford, Iowa, Harvard, Chicago, Yale, and elsewhere — though with the enlargement of the multi-university there is the danger that credit for imaginative creativeness may pass out of sight. Creativity is important in education, as we in our time basically recognize and as Wordsworth well realized. The importance of general imaginative creation, moreover, should not be forgotten. This is a point that is dear to Whitehead also.

The poet thinks of lofty aspiration of wandering scholars of medieval days, but he grants at this point that he may be subjectively idealizing the past too much. It is well, he feels, to be realistic. Even "best things" should not be regarded as "so pure by nature" that they will fulfil to everyone the "highest promise." Nevertheless, he would leave his main criticism of the university standing: he did not love the "guise" of the "scholastic studies" he was required to pursue. Here he re-emphasizes as especially important a point we have mentioned earlier —

> Far more I griev'd to see among the Band
> Of those who in the field of contest stood
> As combatants, passions that did to me
> Seem low and mean . . . (511—)

Wordsworth like many a modern student would have preferred as he says a "freer pace" for his studies. But against the disadvantages of his Cambridge experience we could place the fact that at the university he found a value in seeing more clearly the problems of life in congregated groups. Still, as a student he could observe these problems only in miniature. He realizes, furthermore, that in completing his first year in higher education, he had enjoyed a special privilege in an unjust general social system; in that system many people lacked the barest necessities. Even a most elementary education was not available to them. But the "privileged world" in which he lived while at the university had a virtue, as he explains, because it delayed for him the onset of the greater conflicts of life. It opened up an opportunity in which he could think for a time of many higher things that he would not otherwise have had a chance to contemplate. It is well that at least some people have the leisure to do this.

If college education for Wordsworth had its glories, such as the idealistic ones that have been mentioned, it is also true that in some respects the environment presented the aspect of a comedy. This fact will accord with the experience of many university students at any time. But even such matters as comedy can have a serious value for one who is given to habits of observation, as the poet says. He learned many things even in the "first act" that the comic spectacle presented. There was the opportunity, for example, to study certain of his professors who were "characters" — comparable perhaps to some campus oddities of our own time. Such persons, he tells us, he saw as one might see and study the figures in a puppet show. Nevertheless, the university was in his view "a living part" of an animated totality, a "creek of the vast sea."

What is this vast sea? As Wordsworth is developing his philosophy, may not the vast sea be related to eternity? The poet has been thinking of higher education and his conception of the university may be compared to the living university soul, or spirit, that Whitehead refers to in speaking of the "intertwined group of institutions, the outcome of analogous impulses" greatly extensive in America from Virginia "to Baltimore, from Baltimore to Boston, and from Boston to Chicago." [11] His view of the university spirit is of course far wider than this. It would include education in Paris and in many other cities in the entire world. But Whitehead is well aware of the fact that in particularities the universities tend to fall short of the ideal in various ways. The mental fluctuation in Wordsworth also, as he contemplates the university educa-

84

tion known to him, has been very evident to us all along. Like many a student of our time he was often greatly disturbed by the lack of idealism in high places in the university. As in our own institutions one might frequently see

> Honor misplaced, and Dignity astray;
> Feuds, Factions, Flatteries, Enmity, and Guile;
> Murmuring Submission, and bald Government;
> And Decency and Custom starving Truth;
> The Idol weak as the Idolator;
> And blind Authority, beating with his Staff
> The Child that might have led him . . . (635—)

Nevertheless, for Wordsworth there were always good things available at Cambridge. It would be a mistake to overlook the fact that the university, partaking though it did of certain aspects of a "show," was in reality something far more than any carnival. His education undoubtedly contributed even in his first year to a great expansion of his individuality, as his personal stock-taking, during the summer vacation which followed shortly thereafter, makes clear. This further expansion of the self and Wordsworth's attendant evaluation of his own personality will be examined in the next chapter.

## Footnotes

1. *Adventures of Ideas*, p. 137.
2. *Ibid.*, p. 139. Note the words "some measure"; Whitehead's relativity or relationism is a factor here.
3. *The Aims of Education*, p. 139.
4. *Process and Reality*, p. 268.
5. *Science and the Modern World*, p. 7.
6. *Adventures of Ideas*, p. 29. Consider also Whitehead's reference to "the struggle of novel thought with the obtuseness of language." p. 153. And again, "Language is thoroughly indeterminate . . ." *Process and Reality*, p. 18.
7. John H. Wheelock, *What Is Poetry?* (New York: Charles Scribner's Sons, 1963) p. 40. The idea in this quotation is attributed to Karl Shapiro's *Beyond Criticism* and is found also in Hugo, to whom Shapiro refers.
8. *Ibid.*, p. 39. Wheelock refers to Buber in the essay.
9. *The Aims of Education*, pp. 24, 48.
10. *Ibid.*
11. "Harvard: The Future," *Essays in Science and Philosophy*, (New York, Philosophical Library, 1948), p. 154.

*Interlude*

# A Philosophical Prelude

In speaking of the appreciation of poetry, people often refer to reading poetry as poetry or mention what they call the universe of the poem. Such an approach occurs when their prime purpose is aesthetic, and it presumes a preliminary knowledge of a culture. These preliminaries would include whatever might have been acquired from a background concerning politics, social matters, or religion, whether restrictedly traditional, modernist, or vaguely confused with mores that are a kind of general tone prevailing in one country or another. Along with the ethical factor within a country there is its prevalent aura marked, as Whitehead would say, by its habits of inclusion or exclusion. Many things, such as the paintings and sculptures that pass before the eyes of people, provide a kind of light, or star-circling penumbra which, like the light surrounding a body in the heavens, reaches out widely. And it has its effect upon the response to art or upon the reading of poetry as poetry.

This penumbra is an ever-changing thing which has a certain accordance with the day-to-day reading we do on a variety of subjects, including philosophy, architecture, or whatever we come to know. When in a general book we read passages of poetry we are usually not reading poetry as poetry, but we may later come to read poetry as poetry somewhat better if our casual acquaintance with Plato, Aristotle, Thomas Hill Green, Whitehead, or any thoughtful person we might mention, has been enhanced. Wordsworth and Whitehead are good examples of figures who have added significantly to the wide penumbra by which human beings in the past century or more have been encircled.

The period in which Wordsworth had his early development preceded that in which Whitehead grew up by approximately a decade less than one hundred years. But Wordsworth, even though he is part of an earlier period, saw things in a tightly interwoven relationship much as Whitehead did. The philosopher is deeply concerned about such interrelationships. Certain events in his life as he himself viewed them were remembered as highly interwoven. His youthful period (he was born in 1861) included rumors of war, but it also had its quiet side. Whitehead tells of life in his father's vicarage and of democratic penny readings which he attended in the evenings along with his parents. At times he and his family had the holiday pleasure of traveling abroad to Switzerland and elsewhere on the Continent.

Three early, highly personal experiences made a special impression upon the very young Whitehead. On a certain occasion, as he remembered it, he sat on a bench in a park and saw "a glittering regiment of soldiers" marching past and vanishing "into the unknown." [1] He was then three years old. The memory was vaguely, confusedly, connected with other visions from the world of actuality, but seemed somehow about to be resolved one day by another waking vision, when he was a few years older. This vision occurred in St. James Park, London. In his remembrance "Queen Victoria's Guards" were marching "from the palace." Because of his extreme youth all these things remained blurred in his mind.

The original memory and later associations stayed with him strongly but incomprehensibly (more or less as in a dream) for a decade and a half, until, on a still later occasion when he was walking in a park in Paris, he came to a bench. "The dream that had haunted boyhood was discovered to be a reality held in memory." [2] What had happened in the first instance was that at the age of three he had been taken with his family to Paris and had been present when "the gallant regiments of the French Empire" were starting out on a march "to their doom." The *ending* of "the Napoleonic drama, for which during eighty years Europe was the stage — this final phase, at the glitter of its height and in its downfall, had been flashed" upon him "in two visions of a seat, a palace, and a road." Between the two "visions," Napoleon III had gone into exile, and in this interim had died. These dream-like recollections express something — a small part — of the period of Whitehead's youth.

Are these visions which the philosopher had revelatory? Have they something of the quality of the clairvoyant? Is life itself in his eyes something like a series of dreams? The spectacle of "the glittering regiment" which Whitehead saw at the age of three was connected in the same year not only with other marching forces of men in London but with certain happenings in the same year when, in the United States, "Atlanta was occupied by Union forces, and almost immediately Sherman submitted to Grant his plan for his march from Atlanta to the sea," involving double tragedy. The double tragedy was that of the North and the South.

How do such things in space and time constitute the history that surrounds a human being? Whitehead looks back to their connection with (or relatedness to) the far earlier time of the downfall of the first Napoleon. As an added factor in this large complexity he observes that in England the period in his own life was "marked by the dominance of a small group of liberal aristocrats." All this represents, in symbol, something of his conception of prehension, whereby things are taken together, thought together, and felt together. Togetherness is part of his insight into space, time, and relativity, and relativity is a term

89

which means, for him, more than mere subjectiveness or looseness. Some people think of relativity as a conception that involves the absence of all structure in the world. Not so Whitehead. For him relativity means a complex relatedness or relationism.

We have spoken of a period under the dominance of a small group of liberal aristocrats. Similarly a group of such "liberal aristocrats" dominated the period when the glittering regiments of France vanished into time and when Napoleon III died in exile. In America the double tragedy involving the North and the South also had its relation to a partial liberalism in its various forms: economic and cultural. In the South there was a sense of a putative liberal or democratic culture which had strangely accepted the principle of a fundamental slavery such as existed in classical Greek culture. This may be seen in various writings of the times in the American South.

Whitehead does not speak of the doctrine of classical Greek culture in its relation to the American South, but he is evidently struck by the mystery of things in space and time and their very subtle connection with his personal life. The word "liberal" as Whitehead uses it covers a variety of conceptions — among them actions by Whigs or Tories that have an effect in overthrowing autocratic rule, whether that of Napoleon or any other person. It also has religious connections with a spirit of resistance or opposition to any kind of dominance of the mind from the outside. He had been brought up in England near the narrow waters beyond which were the freedom-seeking Low Countries of Europe, including Holland and Belgium. He refers to them as freedom-seeking. The philosopher's home region partook of the qualities of that region of the liberal Erasmus which is across the slight stretch of seas. "The Narrow Seas," as Whitehead calls them, "are the parents of the free governments of the world," and these governments include "the United States." [3] As to the Narrow Seas he says, "The Pilgrim Fathers were their offspring." Whitehead's early impressions have a relation to the forces that brought liberty to humanity.

We have spoken of visions which were etched upon Whitehead's memory. Still another circumstance in his recollection — a vision, as he views it — is that of the presence of a man, a distinguished visitor in the home of the young boy Whitehead. At the center of the picture as he recalls it is a blazing fireplace. The man before the bright flames was "tall, commanding, stately." [4] He stood "in a genial mood, with his back to the bright fire in the ample hall of the old vicarage house." The great man "is laughing heartily" on being told of a leading parishioner who believed in original sin and "the doctrine of eternal damnation." The figure of the large man, laughing as he stands before the greatly blazing fire, is the boy's remembrance of the very influential Archbishop of Canterbury — the liberal Tait. Is he a kind of Satanic figure in Whitehead's remembrance? The boy had been imbued ambiguously with both conservative and liberal religion.

The term "liberal" has come before us as Whitehead uses it, and we have indicated that it covers a variety of conceptions. It is a word that has application, for instance, to religious doctrine such as was prevalent even in Wordsworth's England of 1800 in which the Calvinist concept of predestination was undergoing change. The modification in the poet's time moved in the direction of a greater measure of free will such as was given acceptance by some members of the Anglican High Church group and was also making its way among Dissenters — a form of modified Calvinism as it came somewhat euphemistically to be called. This background was part of the culture not only of Wordsworth but also of Whitehead's period. It prepared the way for the philosopher's youthful developmental experience.

We have been talking about the combination of time and space: Wordsworth's and that of Whitehead, having a relation not only to England and certain freedom-seeking countries of Europe, but also to America. The conception of time-space as it

91

becomes a thing of coalescence is important in Whitehead. Certain things connected with his reflection and writing were done by him between-times, in various spaces within his home, and — in other moments — in other spaces. Thus in the midst of space-time he carried on his research labor. While he was in England this work was done at times in a library or in a garden. There are reminiscences of his being thus seriously engaged when he was in a garden and quite oblivious of the presence of other people there. At any rate all of this work was done in a state of relationism or relativeness to England and its spaces and times. Then, after 1924, he was in another space-time in America, on the surface of another hemisphere. Perhaps a little imagining concerning Whitehead's period in America will be helpful as we consider this matter of space and time.

At Harvard there is a hall on the front of which is engraved the sentence "What Is Man That Thou Art Mindful of Him?" In the autumn of 1929 I might have been walking down a path toward this hall, carrying in my hand a copy of the Oxford edition of the 1805 *Prelude*, which I had purchased in the Harvard Co-operative Book Store. I am moving, let us say, toward the hall, reading a short passage in the book, and, in doing so, I am moving in space-time, because the space I occupy, for one thing, is almost infinitely changeful. In the upper room at a certain end of the hall, at this very time, Whitehead might have been seated at a table holding in his hand a copy of the 1805 *Prelude* which he also might have purchased at the Harvard Book Store in 1929 or earlier. All this is within the realm of possibility.

As I walk toward the hall I am within the space represented by the yard and the trees and other buildings around me. A child, who is in another space-time, is seated on a green bench, feeding peanuts to a squirrel. Soon she will be walking away on some errand or other in the yard. In a few minutes I will be within the hall, which is within the yard, and shortly thereafter

— as we are imagining things — I will be within a room which is enveloped by the hall. So space, as well as time, may be thought of as disclosing itself to us.

We can think of Whitehead, within the upper room, as he is reading a passage which carries his mind back to earlier times when he had read the poet: at the Sherborne School and at Cambridge. Within his mind at the moment there is the space-time of some of Wordsworth's experiences at school in Hawkshead or at the University of Cambridge in England, where education was important to him. Whitehead could be thinking also of his own writings in which he had referred to Wordsworth. We can see how all these things are examples of inter-relatedness, or relationism. Possibly Whitehead might think of the book *Science and the Modern World* which he had recently examined to correct printer's errors in its first edition. The book *Process and Reality* could have been within his speculation since it carries the very date we are imagining, 1929. In both books he mentions Wordsworth. But enough of present imaginings. The point is that within our actual experience, and within our minds, space-time is very complex. There will be later references and allusions to it in connection with philosophy.

How widely and how relatively Whitehead viewed things is revealed in a late essay, "Harvard: The Future," in which he thinks of the youthfulness of America and contrasts with that youthfulness the age-long development of the university which he, like Wordsworth, attended in Cambridge, England. Far back in 1584 his English university was "grown up." [5] In the one hundred and fifty years that followed this date there occurred a "decisive episode in the drama of human life." Included in that span or space-time were the actions of very influential University of Cambridge men whom he mentions: Spenser, Francis Bacon, Newton, Milton, and Dryden; Cambridge education was important to them. But all of these forces (and these figures were definite forces) became, in effect, not only a part

93

of England but also of America. They constitute part of our culture. The American contribution has grown not from itself alone but from a very wide world, and in the end it becomes supremely important (this idea is Whitehead's) because the center of gravitation "has shifted." We are a part of a new center of gravity. The Western Hemisphere now is a point of reference to the whole world. This was certainly true, economically, when Whitehead was writing, and, if it is less so at present, the political influence is scarcely less powerful.

But to return to the importance of education and Whitehead's essay on "Harvard: The Future." Choose any one of a number of American colleges and universities, thinking even of the place of the industrial arts and technology, and of agriculture in state schools as part of the total ideal of higher training; choose in addition the more general side, the abstract, but never forgetting the importance of innovation — and in the totality of these existential and abstract factors you have a vast enterprise including within it endless varieties of possible and indeed certain measures of actual creativity and relatedness. Whitehead thinks of Chicago, Baltimore, Princeton, Charlottesville in Virginia, and also of Harvard, as part of all this. Any portion may be taken, in reflection, as a vital part — indeed as an entity — symbolic of the other portions which are really but extensions of the vital spirit which is within the whole. Whitehead thinks of this total spirit in relation to mathematics, strangely it may seem, and as connected with Plato.

The span of his thought is often wide. The most important point is that there is something vital to the whole within, or inside, the entirety. Internality must not be forgotten. We in the world have a creative opportunity aiming toward civilization which is "analogous to that of Greece after Marathon, to that of Rome in the reign of Augustus," and to that of whatever constructive values can be conceived in phases of the movements connected with Christian eras (and Hebraic eras), even "amid

94

the decay of civilization." [6] In all these age-long creativities there has been, in a sense, a degree of failure. But always there was shown opportunity in them. For any new day there are renewed sources of hope. As we consider Whitehead's thoughts and words it is as if he were still speaking mysteriously and vitally to us now. Universities, like forms of profound feelings and knowledge, are symbols representing something which is potentially within us all.

### Footnotes

1. "Memories," *Essays in Science and Philosophy* (New York: Philosophical Library, 1948), p. 16.
2. *Ibid.*, p. 17.
3. *Ibid.*, "England and the Narrow Seas," *Essays*, p. 34. For further reference to the life of Whitehead, see "Biographical Comment: Whitehead" below.
4. *Ibid.*, "Memories," pp. 19-20.
5. "Harvard: The Future," *Essays in Science and Philosophy*, p. 153. The growing of a university is part of Whitehead's conception of relativity or relational theory of space and time.
6. *Ibid.*, p. 165.

*Chapter IV*

# Summer Vacation after Wordsworth's First Cambridge Year: Its Relation to Philosophy

At the beginning of Book Four of *The Prelude* we find that Wordsworth has completed his first year at the university and has returned to his home region for the summer vacation. We can pause now for a moment to consider his situation at this stage. In the latter part of the previous chapter we indicated that Wordsworth might possibly have gained more in his first year at college if the Cambridge system had followed the vital "rhythm of education" that Whitehead had referred to in his chapter "The Rhythmic Claims of Freedom and Discipline," which appeared in *The Aims of Education*. Let us recapitulate what had been said earlier and add clarification of a few points.

Whitehead believes that the whole complex rhythm of education is very difficult to achieve because there must be a delicate adjustment of portion to portion in the work done with students. His theory does not suggest that there should be any dictatorial action to accomplish this purpose. Each individual, whether instructor or student, should through his personal philosophy be working toward mutually reinforcing ends. What he is talking about is an ideal. Wordsworth likewise thinks of an ideal as he is contemplating the nature of what education needs to be, if excellence is to be attained. Whitehead indicates it is difficult to know what things in a course of study — say that of mathematics — should receive very strong emphasis. The same problem arises in every field of study in college. Wordsworth does not think of these educational matters in technical language (using the word "rhythm," for example), but essentially he has in mind much the same goal that Whitehead was striving for. Both are, in a sense, poets, or at least they are creative in their feeling for education.

We have said that it is difficult to know what things in a course of study, for example, in mathematics, should receive very strong emphasis. The student, in his imperfect way, has to work this out to some extent. The instructional staff especially needs to consider it. "Surely, in every subject in each type of curriculum," Whitehead writes, "the precise knowledge required should be determined after the most anxious inquiry." [1] But he is skeptical about the actual achievement "in any effective way." The problem of teaching is to be mindful of (1) stimulus, (2) precision, and (3) generalization — seemingly simple things, but complicated at least in their relationships. They are complex, for example, in that while the student is in the first stage, stimulus, with reference to one subject of study he may be in the third stage with reference to another. Wordsworth, we have said, does not consider the matters technically, but he is aware of the fact that *stimulus* was in some way lacking at Cambridge.

The first stage involving stimulus and excitement, which Whitehead earlier refers to as "romantic," might certainly seem to be exceedingly vital — particularly to a person like Wordsworth. But undoubtedly the poet's thought about a university was connected importantly with the other two stages as well. When he himself later taught others he was not unexacting. He knew the meaning of precision. Likewise, in his personal life at least, he recognized the importance of generalization in his own self-education or self-development. The growth of a poet — the over-all theme of his autobiographical remembrances — illustrates this. Generalization, too, is in the background of his stock-taking as he proceeds in the present book of *The Prelude*. The importance of simple delight and of things close to earth could not receive the emphasis which he gave them if he had been lacking in general perception. Likewise his generalizing power is implicit in his sense of the commonalty of man. He does not *think* egocentrically. He thinks of mankind.

In Book Four of *The Prelude* we see the first delight with which Wordsworth returned to his "native hills" and also how he was faced with the problem of trying to recover the past. Even in the simple dwelling where he had lived he savored the past as he turned to the trivial things there which, he tells us, seemed on his return still to be his own. The contrast between "seeming" (Wordsworth's word) — that is, appearance — and on the other hand reality is felt even here. The transiency of all things is also implied at this point in his experience. The "unruly" brook, close at hand, somewhat boxed as it enters and passes through Wordsworth's boyhood garden, is likened to himself. It is called a "child" and is referred to as "froward," but for the moment it is in the close restraint such as a child might be required to feel; its "voice" has been made quiet. The problem of the restricted life and the restrictive environment appears here contrasted with the more open world or environment which Wordsworth had begun to enter through his experience away from home. Again, we find, as we found earlier, that Wordsworth is capable of the double vision: he is serious and yet he smiles. He is providing a "satire" on himself. The brook is a captive, as in a sense he has been; he explicitly says also that it is an "emblem" of his "course of even days"; a less peaceful existence for him now lies ahead.

The first delight with which Wordsworth returned during his vacation to his native hills is signalized further. This delight appears in such simple things as the picture he had of "the snow-white Church upon its hill" sitting "like a thronéd Lady," in the view from his home garden. He feels joy likewise in the pleasure of lying down again in his old bed, "more welcome now" than it would have been — he seems to imply — if at Cambridge he had dwelt upon the subject in sentimental homesickness. The reality — on his return to his boyhood cottage life — might have been a disappointment, through an absurd idealizing which it could have received in his fancy of it. That is, he has been trying to think in a realistic manner. Characteristically the author gives recognition to the small things of life among the villagers, but he observes them in relation to a larger purpose. Some of his friends he

> hail'd
> Far off, upon the road, or at their work,
> With half the length of a long field between. (60—)

There is a homely simplicity, a naturalness, in this moment as it is recaptured in *The Prelude*. This simplicity recalls to mind the openness of character in the man Whitehead. Wordsworth has been speaking of the simple people that he knew well, and it is with these that he felt most comfortable. With certain others he seems to have experienced a kind of constraining effect upon his personality. A very human factor appears in that he felt "pride" and yet, also, some "shame" at the transformation that Cambridge had made in him, as evidenced in his "gay attire." All these happenings are related to the conception of the criticism of human relationships. This criticism of social relations can be connected with the late eighteenth century problem of what Whitehead calls the "status of man" which as the philosopher declared, in thinking about humanitarianism, "required re-considering." [2]

To be critical of the happenings in any period — say in that of the late eighteenth century and the early nineteenth century — is to think in terms of an incipient ideal. This period which pointed toward the development of a new century brought with it an important concern for humanitarianism, the basic theories of which arise as Whitehead views the matter, in the combining of Platonism and a later, developing ideal which was in process over a period of centuries. As we consider society it is possible to "interpret large features of the growth of structure in terms of 'strife.' " [3] Keeping in mind Plato, in contrast to this combativeness, we can "fix attention on the end, rationally worthy"; and Whitehead goes on to explain, in the page that follows, that it is possible to "interpret large features in terms of 'harmony.' " We are faced here with the need of a growth toward what Whitehead later refers to as "respect and friendliness between man and man — the notion of brotherhood." [4] Such emotions even "pervade animal society" and are basic to co-operation and "the urge" which causes us "to help, to feed, to cherish, to play together, to express affection." Whitehead, who is often thought to be entirely esoteric in his philosophy, appears as down-to-earth here as the poet.

Wordsworth, writing in 1805, is a part of the early nineteenth century movement which Whitehead refers to as an important "triumph" in the history of humanity. In Wordsworth and Whitehead there are some reservations concerning the importance of this triumph, but for the moment these may be passed over. Thinking of the faces of humanity, Wordsworth sees them in a wider cosmos, including all animal creation. Among the "faces" that, as he says, he was pleased to see again, there was the face of a dog, the "rough terrier of the hills," now in older age merely a pet in the household of the cottage; by full adoption

> he had pass'd
> Into a gentler service. (90—)

The animal gives service; he is a part of Wordsworth's universe. He is a friend. This "friend" of his earlier rambles had surprisingly been most memorable for having accompanied him on his sojourns when he wrote poetry. When poetical images seemed to come satisfactorily to him (after long and discouraging efforts) often he sprang toward this friend and "let loose" his hand upon the creature's back "with stormy joy"; in his delight in the poetical images he had created, Wordsworth patted the dog madly. Here animal and human world are one. And as we have seen earlier (in the instance of the brook) the poet draws close also to inanimate things. To go on, we find him identifying himself even with a river. It may be startling to think of a person as being like water, but Wordsworth, especially in his capacity as a poet, does not hesitate to think of himself as, in some sense, a "river" — and not only this: he was a river "talking to itself," as in the meantime the dog jogged on ahead.

For Wordsworth the human, animal, and the inanimate world, then, constitute one whole. And the mind of the developing person is a part of this totality. For Whitehead, too, "the brain is continuous with the rest of the natural world." But, for him, as for Wordsworth, even more important is the psychological part of the one-world configuration; it is "an act of self-origination including the whole of nature," [5] though that psychological part is limited, if viewed from one perspective. In writing *The Prelude* Wordsworth too is concerned with self-origination. The point is that many perspectives are necessary, for Whitehead and for Wordsworth. Therein lies the paradox in the effort to understand life, self, and the world. And here

101

past, present, and future (we shall have to refer to future again later) must be included.

Not only this. Wordsworth, in the passage following that which we have just mentioned, was thinking about a former day, now come back to him. And continuing, he tells how on that occasion, but somewhat later in the day when the sun was setting, he left his "cottage door," and, as evening advanced, there came with it a mood of special soberness which led to a form of transmutation of self. Speaking of what he then felt, he says

> Gently did my soul
> Put off her veil, and, self-transmuted, stood
> Naked as in the presence of her God. (140—)

Wordsworth in his summer vacation, then, had undergone a kind of personal moment of self-understanding or perception, and included in it was a sense of peace. It was a moment, he says, in which he felt the necessity of weighing himself, but of doing so in all humility. He saw himself in no specially lofty guise, but in a spirit of self-acceptance and calmness, as well as in a sense of promise. Have we not all on rare occasions felt like this? In his perception he saw far beyond the matters that perish or the things which time imposes upon the self. He had in that moment

> glimmering views
> How Life pervades the undecaying mind,
> How the immortal soul with God-like power
> Informs, creates, and thaws the deepest sleep
> That time can lay upon her . . . (154—)

We are, then, formed not merely by outward forces, but from within, and related to this inwardness, this in-forming, is the creative factor which "thaws" out that aspect of the self which might seem frozen to a state of inertness. Wordsworth has been reflecting on the problem of time, which he has been thinking about in relation to change and, also, in connection with its counterpart in things that are enduring. Man can "daily spread abroad" his selfhood, or that reality which is within the self. In addition to his presentation of such thoughts, peace is again his theme, peace or "pastoral quiet," along with a spirit that possesses what is enduring. Like Wordsworth, Whitehead stresses the importance of inward peace. In addition, he speaks of the humanizing influence of Plato and of the Stoic lawyers in that they point forward toward human rights: "The Stoic lawyers of the Roman Empire introduced a legal reformation largely motivated by the principle that human nature has essential rights." [6] The spearhead of this development of freedom for man appeared later in the new effort of reform with regard to human slavery; earlier the slave trade had been a part of society "as a matter of course."

The thought Whitehead has in mind concerns eventual human brotherhood, an idea which begins to have important developments in the eighteenth century with the doctrine of "the Rights of Man." [7] This we have emphasized earlier. Crucial for our purposes, however, is the fact that "In the last quarter of the eighteenth century, Democracy was born" [8]; and as Whitehead says "it was Democracy" which in the end "freed the slaves." We owe much to past history. Democracy increasingly comes to have a "deeper import" than it had "among the ancients."

The ancients, including the stoic and the Hebraic forces, prepared the way for a new view of man. But Whitehead on the next page comes to "the nineteenth century" and remarks upon its contributions to social-change. In the references to the last quarter of the eighteenth century and to the earlier part of the nineteenth century, Whitehead has come to the important period in the life of Wordsworth, though the poet is not referred to in the context. It is significant, however, that Whitehead near the end of his book connects his thought with a philosophy which includes a theory of peace of spirit which can be won only by "a broadening of feeling" based on "the emergence of some deep metaphysical insight, unverbalized and yet momentous in its coordination of values." [9] The "first effect" of this proper ordering, or combination, is "the removal of the stress of acquisitive feeling arising from the soul's preoccupation with itself."

All these things have analogies, broadly speaking, in Wordsworth. We might question whether Whitehead's word "insight" in the passage quoted has application to the poet in such a context. But Wordsworth did have perception somewhat comparable to the insight Whitehead is talking about. In a spirit of democratic brotherhood the poet sees the human spectacle in the life of those whose very occupations he loved. Through his experiences in his old haunts he found a freshness in human life which he had not fully felt before. Thus he declares

> I read, without design, the opinions, thoughts
> Of those plain-living People, in a sense
> Of love and knowledge; with another eye
> I saw the quiet Woodman in the Woods,
> The Shepherd on the Hills. (203—)

He also saw "with new delight," he says, that simple soul, his "grey-hair'd Dame" (who had been a mother to him when he was a bereft boy); he recognized more deeply her kind affectionateness — a love that was not hampered by "uneasiness" in her dealings with him when he was young. He was drawn to her anew and was warmly disposed even toward the "clear though shallow stream of piety" that she possessed. Such people are the salt of the earth; they are not to be despised merely because of their simple religious tenets. The little things that Wordsworth remembers about this dame-mother became matters of renewed importance when he wrote of them. As he tells

104

> With thoughts unfelt till now, I saw her read
> Her Bible on the Sunday afternoons;
> And lov'd the book, when she had dropp'd asleep,
> And made of it a pillow for her head. (218—)

Wordsworth found that he had attained also in this period a new love of objects, such as "the book," not a love as in the past "in individual happiness," but in a spirit of sharing his joy with other human beings. Nature in his thought was not as yet superseded by man, but his total view was spread more widely over the universe than it had been. Still, mingled with the good, in his new experience, there was also a periodic backsliding or decline; no movement of advance, he realizes, is ever in a continuous unimpeded path. That summer included much "revelry," not particularly because it was pleasing in itself but because he was seeking a new life and freedom; he had not yet found an adequate way to any special goal. The poet even censures himself for the clothes he wore — he re-emphasizes this, having mentioned it earlier. They reflected something of the shallowness of his inner condition. Despite this fact, however, it was during the summer that, though he had made no avowal, he was awakened to a conviction that he would hope to devote himself to some large end — in a word that he

> should be, else sinning greatly,
> A dedicated Spirit. (343—)

We have said in this chapter that Wordsworth reflects on the problem of time which he had been thinking of in *The Prelude* even when he speaks of little things. It is not an absolute time that he has in mind here, but a world of modifications and changes. This is seen early, even when, in speaking of his bed

in the cottage, he indicates how, as a grown person, he nevertheless looked forward and backward in time, and, in the present, took "joy" in the fact that he could lie down at night in
his "accustomed bed" which was

> more welcome now
> Perhaps, than if it had been more desir'd
> Or been more often thought of . . . (73—)

The poet gives pictures of the varying conditions — under
different circumstances in the past — when he looked out of his
bedroom window. Some of these aspects of the changeful world
we have already implied — for example, in the references to the
poet's being like water and like a river. But we see it also in
glimmering views, changes in the weather as it is described,
and changes in the self. He is like a wind. The changes appear
in the midst of weariness, or in self-restoration or "swellings of
the spirit"; they occur in the effect that "time can lay upon" the
self and they operate upon the people around one. There were,
for example, "Babes" Wordsworth "had left" who now, no
longer in arms, were on his return "rosy prattlers," and girls,
who, once seemingly homely, were at the present stage decked
out in the bloom of youthful beauty. On the other hand there
were young people, once attractive, who had lost their charm.
Instances of mutation occur which are likened to the change
that may appear in a garden after one has been absent for so
short a period of time as eight days. There is simple pathos,
which is not immediately apparent, in the factor of change
which manifests itself even to "one who hangs down-bending"
at the side of a boat, satisfying his curiosity with the
"discoveries" that can be made in the deep water. Such a person observes many beautiful things, even in the "weeds, fishes,
flowers"; furthermore, there is the far reach of the phantasy (a
word the poet employs) which can operate in these circumstances. But such a viewer

> often is perplex'd, and cannot part
> The shadow from the substance, rocks and sky
> Mountains and clouds, from that which is indeed
> The region, and the things which there abide
> In their true dwelling . . . (254—)

It is difficult, Wordsworth says, to separate, from various points of view, such tangible things as rocks, and such more tenuous things as the sky as one sees it mirrored in water. And there is the further difficulty of separating from all this the crossing view of the self that one sees as a "gleam" — that is, the crossing view of one's "own image" in the water or indeed of a sunbeam there. In Whitehead's view, comparably, there is a need for "an analysis" which "should find in itself a niche for the concepts of matter and spirit, as abstractions" [10]; in these terms there are still possibilities for the interpretation of experience. To obtain a basis for this analysis the philosopher Berkeley is useful in the criticism which can be directed against the overemphasis on an exclusive sense-orientation. The key to Berkeley's usefulness lies in this respect in an attack upon "the notion of simple location. Berkeley, in effect, criticizes this notion."

Berkeley, as Whitehead explains on the next page, presents a character, Alciphron, who sees at a distance what he regards as a small round tower, but what Euphranor in the dialogue assures him may be seen on a closer view as a "large square building"; Whitehead's interpretation of this incident is not the same as Berkeley's. He presents, rather, as he finally explains, a "provisional realism" [11] which provides a wider perspective of life and the world than Berkeley's. By this approach (which we will not follow here in detail) he leads the way to the philosophy of organism, in which the doctrine of simple location is replaced by a philosophy of perspectivism, interaction, and process. His organic philosophy which brings together into one vast world the totality of past, present, and future has a relationship with the philosophy that Wordsworth is attempting to develop in *The Prelude*.

Whitehead's philosophy includes his presentation of the form of perception which he calls presentational immediacy. We have perception in this form of immediacy if we look, as Wordsworth did, very directly at "weeds, fishes, flowers," noting each one separately. To accomplish this requires strain as Berkeley's character, Alciphron, strains to see the "large square" object which, without the strain, or without a closer view, appears to be round in form. A different kind of perception, according to Whitehead, takes place when we observe something which has reference not to immediacy but to sense experience drawn from the past and related to the present. Later we shall have to say more about this aspect of Whitehead's philosophy which he discusses in the volume *Process and Reality* in a chapter entitled "Strains," and we shall have to say more about simple location, which, as we have just seen, Berkeley had in effect criticized. This merit in Berkeley must be set beside the weakness of his extreme subjectivity.

It was pointed out, a few pages back, that there is a pathos in the element of change which man experiences. But aside from the pains which individuals undergo because of this element of transiency, there is also the problem of world mutation as set against a hope for some possible permanence behind the world of seeming — a seeming which causes distress. This may be observed in many philosophers, and it is evident in Whitehead even when he speaks of "the superior dominance in the consciousness of the contrast" [12] between things which had seemed very different.

The dominance of this "contrast" has led men often to emphasize in their philosophies the changeful, that is, the appearance rather than the deeper reality. Often, as Whitehead says on the next page, "It has had the effect," also, "of decisively separating 'mind' and 'nature' ..." This the philosopher would not wish to do — nor would Wordsworth wish to assert such a separation of mind from nature. There is a relation, furthermore, of the tendency to separate consciousness and the rest of the world in that the individual person needs to deal with the problem of what *appears* to be before him and what is actually there. As Whitehead says on the same page, "The distinction between 'appearance and reality' is grounded upon the process of self-formation of each actual occasion." And this type of self-formation is connected with the construction of our selves. The danger to the self of a too great subjectivity is that we may be *ruled* too often by appearances.

It is this very process of self-formation with which Wordsworth is deeply occupied, not only in the present part of *The Prelude* but in its other books. He is concerned, further, with the union of mind and nature, rather than with their separation. He is interested in the problem of "appearances," but he is more preoccupied with the reality of the external world and the quest for reality that is *beneath* that which is external. Whitehead, however, points out that there are important dichotomies other than the dichotomy of appearance and reality; for example, there is the contrast between "the physical and mental poles, and there are the objects apprehended" as well as "the subjective forms" [13] with their emotional tone determining their power to produce effects in a given occasion of experience.

These other dichotomies are even more important, more basic, than that between appearance and reality. For Wordsworth also this is true. The psychological aspect of these matters and its relation to a deeper insight into *reality* is for him fundamental, though he had, as he admits, found himself full of paradoxes, for he was not merely "solid" but had moments in which he was "light"; he was "short-sighted and profound" — in a word he was *both* "inconsiderate" and thoughtful. Throughout all his fluctuations of thought and feeling he points out, some sixty lines later in the *The Prelude*, a more tragic sense of life (and a deeper sense of brotherhood) was near at hand. On one occasion during the summer, while walking in happiness and moonlit solitude — feeling an almost "animal delight" in nature — he came upon an old soldier in faded uniform —

> A man more meagre, as it seem'd to me,
> Was never seen abroad by night or day.
> His arms were long, and bare his hands; his mouth
> Shew'd ghastly . . . (408—)

This specter-like soldier had seen service in the tropic islands, had returned to England, and, having been dismissed from the army, was making his way toward his home. The hour being late, and no nearby villager stirring, Wordsworth took his companion back by the road a short distance to the home of a laborer he knew. There the young Wordsworth was able to obtain for the traveler a night's lodging and much needed food. It was, as we may say, an act expressive of the poet's belief in the importance of man as a person valued in and of himself — that is, of faith *in* his fellow man and in the value of the world. A philosophy which would present us with a fragmented, or an atomistic world stands, if consistent, opposed to this. In the century previous to that of Wordsworth's great achievement, the philosopher Hume had been ruled by such a fragmented view and it was probably because of this fragmented outlook that Hume could say that "there is no such passion in human minds, as the love of mankind, merely as such. . . ." [14]

The acceptance, on the other hand, of the world and of its significance as a grand totality, includes in Wordsworth an acceptance of oneself. It reveals his faith in himself. This faith is noninductive. For Whitehead similarly a belief in a self that reaches out most widely is not validated by any "inductive process." [15] It is a faith, rather, which grows from "our own immediate experience." For as he says, "There is no parting from your own shadow." All this involves a belief, a faith, that Wordsworth was also coming increasingly to possess. But Whitehead's faith should be noted. "To experience this faith," Whitehead says, "is to know that in being ourselves we are more than ourselves: to know that our experience, dim and fragmentary as it is, sounds the utmost depths. . . ." Such a belief, for him includes a sense of the harmony of all things — including in that harmony aesthetic values.

For Wordsworth the act of aiding the gaunt soldier from the tropic islands was not in itself a thing to be greatly magnified. But in another sense it did sound certain depths of reality having a pertinence to a summer vacation which was yet more than a "vacation." It was a time having a vital importance to his life. Helping the soldier was a simple and natural act, but its significance to Wordsworth is emphasized by his placing it in the terminal, climactic position in the present account of his summer. We do not see the total psychological experience that Book Four of *The Prelude* represents if we are without knowledge that his philosophy is growing.

Wordsworth was not merely presenting a simple personal recollection of events. He was progressing in his self-understanding beyond the stage developed in the previous book concerning his first Cambridge year. His philosophy was broadening. Undoubtedly an increased knowledge of books which he had read contributed to this widened understanding. He had not, however, focused attention upon books in this part of *The Prelude* or in previous parts. It is to the subject of books that he wished next to turn as we shall see in the following chapter.

## Footnotes

1. *The Aims of Education*, p. 56.
2. *Adventures of Ideas*, p. 36.
3. *Ibid.*, p. 39.
4. *Ibid.*, p. 46.
5. *Ibid.*, p. 290.
6. *Ibid.*, pp. 16-17.
7. *Ibid.*, p. 22.
8. *Ibid.*, p. 23.
9. *Ibid.*, p. 367.
10. *Science and the Modern World*, pp. 97-98.
11. *Ibid.*, p. 100; see also p. 102, p. 103, and especially p. 107 where he refers to "memory of the past, immediacy of realisation, and indication of things to come." Earlier, Whitehead, in his *Principles of Natural Knowledge*, had quoted from Berkeley's *Principles of Human Knowledge*. Evidently, he was much impressed by Berkeley.
12. *Adventures of Ideas*, p. 268. See also p. 269.
13. *Ibid.*, p. 268; see also the comment on "prehension," p. 227.
14. As quoted by Whitehead in *Ibid.*, p. 37.
15. *Science and the Modern World*, p. 27.

*Second Interlude*

# Brief Biographical Comment: Wordsworth

In our "Introduction" and in "A Philosophical Prelude" only a few matters were mentioned about Wordsworth's life. Here we may say that an interesting thing about the central feature of Wordsworth's main work in his great period (1797-1812) is that, after the French Revolution occurred, he occupied himself with a problem that might in our day be dealt with psychoanalytically. He had been confronted, for a time, with a situation where nothing seemed worthwhile. The most important work in which this problem is faced is *The Prelude*; it is dealt with in the latter part of the poem. What is it about this poet's life that can explain, to some degree, the circumstances of a person who was dealing with such a serious psychological question, the kind of situation which, if not dealt with, might lead to suicide? His problem was basically religious and philosophical. It concerned an outlook which, as it developed, came to be regarded as *experiential*. Can we say that any one of us can possibly find religion, not institutionally, but through experience, or through experiences? It was through his experiential ongoing life that Wordsworth found his way out of the difficulty that he was faced with. This we shall speak of later.

Wordsworth was born in 1770 in Cockermouth, Cumberland,

in the Lake District of Northwest England, not far from the Irish Sea. The border of Scotland was some twenty-five miles north of where he lived. His mother, who had an influence upon his basic seriousness and his self-identity, died in 1777, and his father died in 1783. Losing his mother when he was seven and, a few years later, losing the father — who had brought to him a love of Spenser, Shakespeare, and Milton — could not have failed to strike him traumatically. Undoubtedly his early experiences of shock contributed to the seriousness of his outlook and his increasingly troubled feeling about the nature of the world.

In his extreme youth he was educated at home by his father. After his parents died the boy was placed under the indirect control of relatives. He was then fourteen. As was often the case with youths in England, the most direct influence upon his life at this time was given in school. He received his continuing education at Penrith (the place of his mother's rearing) and at Hawkeshead, where he lived in the home of a dame mother. At Hawkeshead he was under Newtonian influence.[1] The kind of family from which he came is revealed somewhat in that his father had been an attorney, and his older brother Richard went to London and became a successful lawyer. Another brother, Christopher, finally attained the position of Master of Trinity College, Cambridge. An uncle on his mother's side had the position of Fellow at Cambridge University, and Wordsworth was given a scholarship there in 1786. But while at college he spent more time in his own musings than in diligent student effort, and thus fell somewhat short of the family tradition. We shall have more to say later of Cambridge University and Wordsworth's situation there.

We are involved in this volume with an inquiry into the ideas of Wordsworth and Whitehead and the interrelationship between the two men, together with the possible influence that the poetry of *The Prelude* may have had on the reflection of Whitehead. All of this material cannot, however, be fully ex-

114

perienced if the personalities and the historical background of these two figures are not taken into account. What was the character of the period in which Wordsworth lived? There was at that time a situation of social and political imbalance in England. Whitehead's friend Elie Halévy has thought carefully about the time and its later outgrowths, and he holds that it is a grave danger "for a nation to sacrifice its agriculture to the development of its industries"; ought we not to regard it as "perilous," he asks, as he thinks of England, for any country "to become dependent upon the foreigner for the satisfaction of its most elementary needs?" [2] This we now know was the situation developing around 1805 in Wordsworth's great period. It did not come definitely to a head for general consideration until a decade later, but all along it was a matter of moment.

The possibility of imbalance in a nation, as between agriculture and industry, at that time was only one part of the danger of disorganization in England and in the world. In addition to social, political, and aesthetic manifestations — along with the economic factors we have just mentioned — there was an extreme religious ferment connected with developments in science. These developments involved getting rid of what Whitehead later referred to as an extreme of the eighteeenth-century doctrine based on highly-stressed "common sense." [3] This eighteenth-century perspective, Whitehead says, "had got rid of 'medieval phantasies,' " and here he speaks ironically. In effect he was criticizing our own tendency today which often involves a pedestrian common sense outlook placing great stress upon the material world to our own detriment. But his main intent is to criticize the materialism that was rampant in the highly rationalistic eighteeenth-century period. The extreme of eighteenth-century common-sense reflection Whitehead sets beside certain almost equally primitive philosophical ideas of Descartes, which concerned one vortex or another whirling as a part of a vast co-ordination whereby an attempted unification of the world was conceived. Philosophical ideas of the latter kind were then thought of in connection with science. The vortices were presumed to co-ordinate the rotation of planets and the rotation in matter. Religion and science were at odds subsequently to the time of Descartes. Both, according to Whitehead's view, were unduly simplistic. But the religious ferment had its value in opening a way to theological liberalism. Like a yeast it was pervasively in action among the Church of England Evangelicals, the Presbyterians in Scotland and elsewhere, the Baptists, the Methodists, and the Quakers. To give only one example, most of them, and some Catholics, were sharply stirred up about abolition. Hoping to aid them in their cause concerning Negro freedom, which had begun to have deep religious involvement, there were among the Dissenters, as Halévy says, "many Rationalists, some who were practically Deists." [4] Interest in this problem concerning slavery extended far beyond England to Africa, Spain, France, and even to Vienna. "In the United States the abolitionist movement was born of an alliance between the Quakers and the adherents of natural religion, Franklin, Tom Paine, and their disciples." Thus religious radicals and secular humanitarians were brought together over the abolition problem.

Wordsworth was concerned about this matter and about economic imbalances, and the relation between such imbalances and potential troubles with other nations. He was stirred up also about additional social evils. Problems of religion in the strict sense were likewise actively in his mind. Wordsworth changed as the period in which he lived underwent change. The spirit of religious and social liberalism in his work of the great period stands out in strong contrast to his final hardening into conservatism, which is reflected in the very late 1850 version of *The Prelude*. By omitting or ignoring certain passages or phrases in this late edition, the poem can be read (and has often been read) without a sense of its being contradictory to the spirit characterizing his writing in the earlier

116

period when he was a liberal. The work by Wordsworth that affected Whitehead, however, was that which represented the poet's most marked creativity in thought.

The philosopher was not in the end influenced, then, by Wordsworth's later conservatism. But something further must be said about linkages in Wordsworth's background. To understand him more fully it is necessary to realize that he was affected to some extent by the dominant tendency of the century preceding his birth — a period which goes back to the time of Dryden's greatest poetry and that of subsequent English writers who were under Dryden's influence. Of these authors there was one poetical figure whom Wordsworth's father regarded so highly that he had his son memorize passages of the poet's work. That writer was the neoclassicist Alexander Pope. Those reacting against Dryden and his direct successors, however, constituted a group which had the greatest final effect upon the poet. Wordsworth did not aim primarily at the graceful, the elegant, and the highly concentrated in poetry that had been predominantly fashionable. Such qualities, associated with much eighteenth-century poetry, Wordsworth, in general, abhorred. His poetry, in contrast, often leads into endless vistas and can at times have a quality of thinking aloud. Also it has, on other occasions, a colloquial and abrupt character such as is observed in speech which is not premeditated.

Wordsworth does not write a poem for the mere delectation of an eighteenth-century gentleman who would not stoop to have a dialogue or to argue about anything in an unseemly or ill-considered manner. He was not gentlemanly in this sense. He was close, however, to the tender late eighteenth-century poetry of William Cowper and of Burns. Both Cowper and Burns, though lesser poets, had a positive effect on the young Wordsworth. Burns's "John Anderson My Jo" or his "Highland Mary" undoubtedly had an appeal for Wordsworth, as had William Cowper's "Light Shining out of Darkness" or the

117

passage from his poem *The Task* (Book II) where, as an outsider thinks of the case of the Negro, he realizes that in the relation between White and Black

> brotherhood is sever'd as the flax
> That falls asunder at the touch of fire.

Science and mathematics were offered at the University of Cambridge when Wordsworth was there, whereas at Oxford that side of the curriculum had not been developed. But in the years when Wordsworth was a student at Cambridge, mathematics was taught in a manner approximately one hundred years behind the times. The instruction in that decade, according to Elie Halevy, had not reached much beyond the 1689-1699 fluxion period of Newton. Methods of mathematical thought of the late seventeenth and early eighteenth century were "obstinately maintained." [5] Wordsworth greatly admired the achievements of Newton, and it would seem therefore that the study of mathematics should have attracted the poet. Much was undoubtedly lacking in clarity, however, when the instructors attempted the explanation of "fluents" and their "fluxions" which Newton had represented by a letter with a dot over it. The fluxions concerned a flowing action and variations in movement.

Wordsworth at an early stage had a sense of the potential dynamism within the movement or the flowing action of a wheel — a dynamism which he could sense even while looking at the wheel while it was at rest, and he was capable of likening that wheel, at the point of rest, to nature in certain of her extremely quiet but incipiently dynamic moments. This he perceived in a sonnet of 1786 that carries as a title "Written in Very Early Youth." The poem was probably composed in his last year as a student at Hawkeshead. But more will be said later about Wordsworth's life in the period of his college years. Undoubtedly he was disappointed with some of the offerings at

Cambridge, though it must be mentioned to the credit of the university that for twenty or more years "Cambridge had been distinguished by its zeal for the abolition of the slave trade." [6] Change was in the air. Enthusiasm for the French Revolution was manifested at Cambridge.

At the close of the poet's third college year, in 1789, he went to France on a vacation. Later, after graduation — when once more in France — he entered into a relationship with Annette Vallon, who was four years his senior. By her he had a child, Caroline. It seems he intended marriage (planning to obtain money in England) but, on his return to his homeland, finances were not forthcoming. War between France and England intervened and continued for some ten years. Change as well as revolution was in every breath of his life. He sent money for the support of Caroline and went to France finally to visit with Annette — perhaps to explain his later situation more fully to her — prior to his marriage with Mary Hutchinson, which took place in October 1802. Subsequently Wordsworth provided money for his daughter Caroline's dowery.

The decade and a half of the poet's greatest work, beginning about 1797, followed the inception of *Lyrical Ballads*, which he produced with Coleridge. This book was not devoted exclusively to lyrical ballads. The nature of the volume may be seen by reading the "Preface" of its second edition (written by Wordsworth) and also noting the non-ballad character of the work. This non-ballad feature takes on a meditative quality. It is evident in the earlier and later editions of *Lyrical Ballads*, and is notable in the poem "Tintern Abbey."

Some of Wordsworth's best works which followed — including short portions of *The Prelude* and also the Lucy poems — were composed in the winter at the close of 1798 in Germany, and in early 1799. In the period following 1801, under the inspiration of a reading of Milton, he wrote in a form which he later referred to as a nun's "narrow room"; this was his brief description of the sonnet. In his development of this

119

highly concentrated form of poetry he became one of the greatest sonneteers ever to write in English.

When we think of Milton we usually remember a kind of marathon or long-running power which he possessed, and Wordsworth in *The Prelude* has something of this same almost obsessive marathon quality. But both writers also attained great control over the sonnet, the concentrated form which, as Wordsworth says, Tasso in the course of his life produced and reproduced until he had written it a thousand times. Wordsworth himself was perhaps trying to show his mettle when he wrote over five hundred poems in this restricted form. This, like Tasso's achievement, is a marathon quality of a sort. In "Scorn Not the Sonnet," however, Wordsworth thinks especially of Milton who, though he could make of the sonnet a veritable "trumpet," through it

> blew
> Soul-animating strains — alas, too few!

Wordsworth died in 1850 when he was eighty years old. His influence was extensive in the first quarter of the nineteenth century but equally great in the expanse of time extending from the years after his death down to 1900. Byron, who had satirized Wordsworth early, came to admit the injustice of his satire (Byron used the word "unjust" in reference to it), and he later wrote passages in *Childe Harold's Pilgrimage* which show the influence of Wordsworth. In the poem Byron says — in speaking imaginatively of his self-representative character — that for him lofty "mountains are a feeling" (Canto Three, Stanza 72). Here he speaks almost with the tone of Wordsworth. Byron's passages are, it is true, highly rhetorical, whereas Wordsworth's are not, but many readers have been brought, through Byron, to an appreciation of serious aspects of Wordsworth which they might otherwise have missed.

120

## Footnotes

1. See footnote 8 (Moorman) and following context material in our Chapter Two.
2. *A History of the English People in the Nineteenth Century, I, England in 1815*, translated by E.I. Watkin and D.A. Barber (New York: Barnes and Noble, Inc., 1961), p. 203. The material in Halevy is italicized.
3. "Relativity," *Science and the Modern World*, p. 166. Note also a comment on Whitehead's "relational theory of space" by Northrop in *The Philosophy of Alfred North Whitehead*, ed. Paul Arthur Schilpp (La Salle, Illinois: Open Court, 1971) p. 175; criticisms of the theory are "exceedingly artificial."
4. *A History of the English People in the Nineteenth Century*, I, p. 458.
5. *Ibid.*, p. 549. Fluxions were derivatives or rates of change.
6. *Ibid.*, p. 548.

# Brief Biographical Comment: Whitehead

Understanding what is involved in Wordsworth's thought as related to that of Whitehead required a number of preliminaries, which were treated in our introductory material; here it may be helpful to think, in summary, of the scope of the philosopher's career. Alfred Whitehead was born in southeast England in 1861 in a town on an isle in the county of Kent. It seems clear that he was a descendant of a Quaker, named Whitehead, of earlier days. In any event he was definitely influenced by the Quaker religion. Before he left home for school, at the age of fifteen, he had known well the provincial figures of his region. Close to his home was the village of Minster at a spot where Augustine, while in England, "preached his first sermon." [1] At a little distance from this village is the town of Sandwich which in Whitehead's youth still retained "its Flemish houses lining the streets." It had been originally settled by people from the Low Countries across the water. In 1875 Whitehead was entered in School at Sherborne, in Dorset, directly west at the other end of England from the place where he was born. It was in this Dorset region that Coleridge and Wordsworth, three-quarters of a century before, had done collaborative writing. The poetry of Wordsworth had a profound effect on Whitehead early and late. This influence was especially strong in the philosopher's days at Sherborne and in his life following his preparation for Cambridge. At the university he studied four years as an undergraduate and then did three years of graduate study before attaining his Fellowship. While there he also read Wordsworth.

Whitehead's youthful time was preceded by that in which the young Wordsworth grew up by about ninety years. The two periods had certain similarities, as we shall see, in that they both represent progressive developments, or steps leading toward a somewhat intricate liberal interrelationship. This is not surprising since the later period in these respects developed out of the earlier one. Religious factors of an experiential nature were important in the two figures. In this connection it is of interest to recall that Whitehead has referred to "the present immediacy of a kingdom not of this world." [2] The theme in his mind includes allusion to the ideal, to something unworldly; the reference is not to anything mundane. But the word "present" in the passage we have quoted might have been underlined and, perhaps even more important for stress, there is the word *immediacy*. The experience is psychologically immediate. Of course the concept of present experience needs to be interpreted. But the human adventure is significant here. We do have experiences in it with regard to the ideal.

Whitehead's personal life is greatly helpful in understanding his nature. Five years after he received his fellowship and his teaching position at Cambridge, he and young Evelyn Wade were married. This was in 1890. To her he later dedicated his book *The Principle of Relativity* in these words in the fly-leaf: "To my wife whose encouragement and counsel have made my life's work possible." Her effect upon his "outlook on the world" was, as he elsewhere declares, "so fundamental, that it must be mentioned as an essential factor" [3] in his philosophic production. She helped also in the broadening of his religious outlook. Through her he came to hold that "beauty, moral and aesthetic, is the aim of existence"; from her he learned, indeed, that "kindness, and love, and artistic satisfaction" are among the modes of the very attainment of moral and aesthetic beauty. It is the ideal, not the materialistic, which in Whitehead is most important.

John Henry Newman, despite his belligerence on certain points, had been an influence working subtly within the mind of Whitehead, very possibly due to Newman's emphatic criticism of any idolatrous worship of a book and because of the firm case which he made for the importance of the long historical development of religion. For a period during Whitehead's later work as a student he was drawn toward the claims of an authority-religion, but his association with Evelyn Wade was a factor in his change from this tendency. Bertrand Russell says — possibly with exaggeration — that Whitehead "was only turned aside at the last minute by falling in love with her." [4] Thereafter he was unwilling to be confined to any official religious system, though he continued to feel reverence for the immense historical perspective of the religions of East and West, and he felt, as Newman felt before 1845, that Anglicanism is what one theologian has called a world in itself. The extreme tenderness of Newman, despite a certain surprising bellicosity, may also have influenced the philosopher and may have done its work in combination with the humanity of Wordsworth.

Many students have borne testimony to the generosity of Whitehead, both as a man and as a teacher. He gave help to students I myself have known who were in financial need, sometimes perhaps beyond the point of wisdom in view of his own circumstances. He was, moreover, most modest before his students and before others about any achievement he might have made. This modesty, according to Bertrand Russell, went along with a tendency to be strongly appreciative of others. Russell's judgment was that Whitehead was "extraordinarily perfect as a teacher." [5] As Russell goes on to say, Whitehead would "elicit from a pupil the best of which a pupil was capable. He was never repressive, or sarcastic, or superior, or any of the things that inferior teachers like to be." Russell closes on the note that Whitehead inspired in his finest students a "lasting affection."

The Whiteheads had two sons and a daughter, all of whom served in World War I. Their son Eric was shot down in a plane on the front in 1918. The effect on Whitehead was traumatic but he continued his philosophical ponderings perhaps because of the distress he felt. Wordsworth similarly worked on reflective problems in a period of trauma which he underwent. But to return to Whitehead's earlier situation. Eight years after his marriage he published his mammoth *Treatise on Universal Algebra* on which he had labored beyond the commonplaces of the subject for seven years. This was in 1898. Immediately after completing it he began studies somewhat more broadly for a second volume on the subject, but he changed his plans, and while still teaching, he undertook the task of the first volume of *Principia Mathematica*. This work — which extended mathematics further beyond the commonplace and the consideration of ordinary quantity — he dwelt upon for a long period in collaboration with his former student, Bertrand Russell. Each would work on the basic problems separately and then they would confer. Russell has told how he submitted a portion of the book to Whitehead, who, being dissatisfied, wrote in reply: "Everything, even the object of the book, has been sacrificed to making proofs look short and neat." [6]

In this situation Russell had been guilty, he himself says, of a fault "due to a moral defect" in his "state of mind." This is Russell's own almost humble self-evaluation; his modesty at this point is notable. The ideas for the volume took some ten years in the process of elaboration. In order to bring the material to the Cambridge University Press when it was published in 1911 there were so many sheets in large script that it was necessary to hire a cabby with his "old four-wheeler" [7] to provide for its transportation. An expert scholar has called it "one of the great intellectual monuments of all time" [8]; it should be said that in regard to the division of labor carried on by the two authors the ideas in every sentence of the whole long book represented in Whitehead's words a collaboration. The contribution of each thinker intimately interacted with that of the other.

Often philosophers have thought of Whitehead solely as a master of high abstractions in mathematics and philosophy. It is true that he was most exceptional in these fields, but as we have seen he was deeply concerned about the individual personally and about social and political liberties. His "opinions" even in his University of Cambridge days, were, as he explained, "on the liberal side, as against the conservatives." [9] Had he remained in England he would have voted in later days "for the moderate side of the Labour Party." As a political speaker, or as a leader on the platform with others, he at times underwent the indignity of having old eggs and oranges hurled at him. According to his own words he was often "covered by them." All this he took in stride as a necessary part of the activity of living according to his ideals.

At Cambridge, the Whitehead family enjoyed the development of many friendships, among them that of Elie Halévy and his wife. Halévy, whom we have earlier quoted about historical background in a variety of ways (in the "Biographical Summary: Wordsworth"), spent much time in England because he was engaged in research for his monumental work on nineteenth century history. Quotations we have made from his work have especial importance in view of the close connection he had with Whitehead both in Paris and in England. The two men shared many ideas. They were strikingly individual, however, and the uses they made of the facts about England were by no means identical. Still, there was what Whitehead would call a relationism between them. Their relation involved

126

a profound psychological interaction.

Whitehead's Cambridge period, subsequent to his attainment of a fellowship and his being given a university teaching position, extended for twenty-five years down to 1910, when he and his wife left their home and took residence in London. He had no job at this time; the change was a venture. After completing a new volume, entitled *An Introduction to Mathematics*, he was offered a position teaching in University College, London. This was in 1911. Three years later he was given a professorship in London at the Imperial College of Science and Technology. While continuing this work he was appointed to the chairmanship of "the Academic Council which manages the internal affairs concerned with London education" [10]; this was a totally new experience which brought a transformation in his outlook and made him far more aware of general problems in the modern world than he had ever been while teaching at Cambridge.

Whitehead achieved his first philosophical renown most particularly because of four books which he wrote in his London period: *The Aims of Education* (1916), *The Principles of Natural Knowledge* (an Enquiry), *The Concept of Nature*, and *The Principle of Relativity*. On the completion of a residence of some fourteen years in London, he was invited by Harvard University to come to America, and he decided to accept the invitation because of the great freedom which it made possible to him for new work. He was to be permitted an opportunity of offering any courses he wished on his own developing philosophy. He and his wife came to Harvard in 1924. Again, as in the case of his moving to London, his further removal to America added to his liberalism and his sense of what he regarded as interrelation.

His fame had traveled before him, meanwhile, because of the four books that have just been mentioned. The last one, *The Principle of Relativity* (1922), was perhaps most profoundly suggestive of what he was next to accomplish. The philosopher

127

gave much thought at this time to the question of the strife between religion and science. He personally refers to it as a strife. It presents at any rate a problem which he incorporated in *Science and the Modern World*, written in his early days at Harvard. It has connection also with certain of his other later works. To suggest the scope of Whitehead's thought in this final period we will mention a number of other books that he wrote. *Religion in the Making* (1926) was followed by seven important volumes: *Symbolism, Process and Reality, The Function of Reason* (delivered as lectures at Princeton), *Adventures of Ideas, Nature and Life* (presented first at the University of Chicago), *Modes of Thought*, and *Essays in Science and Philosophy*. This last was prepared for the press in 1947. All of these volumes are connected with Harvard and are among his most penetrating works. The very titles themselves are suggestive of his interests. He died at the age of eighty-six on December 30, 1947.

## Footnotes

1. Whitehead, "Autobiographical Notes," in *The Philosophy of Alfred North Whitehead*, edited by Paul Arthur Schilpp (La Salle: Open Court, 1971), p. 4. The "Autobiographical Notes" may be found with slight typographical changes in *Essays in Science and Philosophy*. See p. 8.
2. *Process and Reality*, p. 520. Our "Brief Biographical Comment: Wordsworth" deals with the liberal religious background of Wordsworth's time. See also "A Philosophical Prelude" for important material concerning Whitehead's background.
3. "Autobiographical Notes," in volume edited by Schilpp, p. 8.
4. *The Autobiography of Bertrand Russell, 1872-1914*, p. 190. See also p. 226.
5. *Ibid.*, p. 191. See also p. 190 concerning Whitehead's modesty.
6. *Ibid.*, p. 227.
7. *Ibid.*, p. 229.
8. Willard V. Quine in *The Philosophy of Alfred North Whitehead*, p. 139.
9. "Autobiographical Notes," p. 13.
10. *Ibid.*, p. 11.

*Chapter V*

# Stored Learning: Books as Related to Wordsworth and Whitehead

In the previous chapter we noticed the self-revelation of *The Prelude* in Wordsworth's Book Four account of the summer vacation after his first year at the university. This vacation had given him an opportunity to take stock of himself and, in his continuing individual appraisal later in the poem, he expanded in part unconsciously his personal introspection further. The danger of an unfortunate egoism through such a preoccupation is evident. Self-revelation is, however, a definite part of the literature of expansiveness, as we have already suggested, and it has its reason for being. We, as readers, understand ourselves better through the self-disclosure which poets or other writers have given. In the case of Wordsworth we understand his philosophy better after reflecting on what he says when he speaks more personally.

The poet felt that he had greatly extended the record of his

130

life, and he decided to round off his story by writing Book Five on the subject of the stored or recorded learning of human beings and how it deserves to be valued. This valuation of reading had a connection with his previous university experience and with his summer spent in attaining an intellectual self-review. But, apart from books, the unconscious influence of external nature upon him continued all along to be exceedingly great. What concerns him, apart from telling the story of his life, is his world-view, which includes nature and its potentiality as an influence on man. But he was aware that the reader of his poetry, unless forewarned, might conclude that books were of negligible significance in his early outlook upon life.

In beginning Book Five Wordsworth tells us that he feels acutely, as do many socially-oriented writers, about the condition or state of mankind and its woeful aspects. Such is the feeling of certain authors today, such as Michael Novak, who would single out gleams of hope for us in a generally darkened sky. But the poet says that he is struck chiefly not by the woes of mankind, though these are vast; most surprisingly, the thing that comes immediately to his mind is the pathos which strikes him as he thinks of the achievements that have been made. Here he is approaching philosophy. Looking at the human race in our time would we say there is also something of pathos which we could feel as we consider the scientific and other gains in the modern world?

For Wordsworth everything that has been produced through art and knowledge has its peculiar implicit pathos, most especially because it must in the end vanish. Indirectly he is thinking also of the mystery of time and change. Somewhat parallel to Wordsworth's thought, concerning permanence and impermanence, is Whitehead's idea that "the higher intellectual feelings are haunted by the vague insistence of another order, where there is no unrest, no travel, no shipwreck. . . ." [1] For Whitehead, as he says on the next page, a truly fundamental evil in the world "lies in the fact that the past fades, that time is a 'perpetual perishing.' " On the next following page he explains that our cosmology must include "the final opposites, joy and sorrow, good and evil, disjunction and conjunction . . ."

But should we say that personal tragedies are less to be lamented, as Wordsworth seems to suggest, than the intellectual and artistic losses that people may suffer? Why does the poet grieve less for all the entangled human woes, the keenly tragic personal experiences, and more for the loss of artistic and scientific productions? Is he, for the moment, far from a philosophy that emphasizes personalism? The explanation with respect to Wordsworth, it would seem, is that he is thinking of books: that art and knowledge represent, for him, not a mere transitoriness but a profound reality much as "the ideas" represented a reality for Plato, whose conceptions, as explained by Whitehead, receive " 'life and motion' by their entertainment in a living intelligence. Such a living intelligence with its 'gaze fixed upon ideas' was what Plato termed a Psyche, a word we can translate as 'soul.' " [2]

This Platonic theory — which is to be differentiated in certain ways from the more or less conventional religious theory of the soul — has a very wide aspect even in its manifestations among human beings in the world. In its human and other relations, as Whitehead explains in the context from which we have quoted, it participates in "a basic Psyche whose grasp of ideas conditions impartially the whole process of the Universe." But the soul-grasp of ideas referred to here does not include a grasp of "mere knowledge, that is to say, of mere understanding"; it rises above what in general is achieved in an "age of professors," and for Whitehead it involves a quality of love. This love — the "Eros" — is an active force. Whitehead himself finds an inspiration in Plato in this respect. The conception of this operative force is related also to ideas found in certain modern psychologists, for example, in Erich Fromm.

Such a love involves even the profitable use of books.

Art and knowledge, we have suggested, represented also for Wordsworth not a mere transitoriness but a profound reality or, as in the case of the Platonic ideas, a life, or an almost animated being. In the poet's view, the works of man contain something immortal, and yet, paradoxically, so far as we can tell they will ultimately vanish — be known no more. There is a parallel here to the problem of the mortality of man and his desire for immortality. What can we say of the being of man, idealistically or realistically conceived, when we realize that a time will come when he will no longer need the works of art and science that man has produced? If he could have an existence without possessing such things, what kind of existence would it be? Wordsworth is faced with the old problem of material and immaterial reality. Here we have a phase of philosophy.

Continuing, the poet contemplates the possibility that all human art and science might in some cataclysm be destroyed, and yet life — reduced to a state lower than that of the animal — might survive. Thinking of the creative fecundity of the universe, he conceives that the human being, even without books or other arts, would slowly rise again. It is his belief that even in the event of world-wide fire, the "living Presence" in the universe would still be eternally at work, "composure would ensue"; thus humanity would find a "presage sure," pointing beyond the midnight of destruction toward "a returning day." Thinking of this problem, and books, Wordsworth asks:

> Oh! why hath not the mind
> Some element to stamp her image on
> In nature somewhat nearer to her own?
> Why, gifted with such powers to send abroad
> Her spirit, must it lodge in shrines so frail? (44—)

Answering this, *The Prelude* shows that there is such "an element" or medium with which to work: human beings themselves. This is implied in the poem. The literary productions of Wordsworth and other poets, or of authors of fiction, are in the end not only in the medium of words but are a form of consciousness; they are part of an age-long process. An artist's true work is done in the medium of life far more importantly than in his artifacts, which of course may vanish at any time. The whole problem that Wordsworth is treating here — that of his conception of the goal of man's striving — looks forward to the poet's "Immortality Ode."

Wordsworth attempts to clarify things concerning books through telling of a dream which a "friend" of his had. In it we see an Arab, lost in a desert waste, carrying two objects. One of these, under his arm, was a stone; the other, clutched in his hand, was a shell. The first is a symbol of the ideal aspects of mathematics (or science) and the second, which "was a God, yea, many Gods," is representative of poetry having, it seems, a philosophic character. We learn that the value of the "stone" is almost inestimable, but according to Wordsworth the "shell," associated more immediately as it is with life, is of even "more worth." The dream was one which he himself actually had.

The shell and the stone together constitute something like the philosopher's operative "Eros," or the creative force, a "Craftsman" which Whitehead adapts for the purpose of his own philosophy. Plato we have seen is his source. There is an element of humor, yet a profound seriousness in Plato's thought about this "Craftsman." In the page of *Adventures of Ideas* from which we last quoted, the "Eros" is represented as the activity of soul in its enjoyment and in its creative achievement. It functions spiritually in the world, but it is not omnipotent.

Whitehead stresses the point concerning the absence of omnipotence in the "Eros"; he suggests that Plato "should have written" a dialogue on the opposing forces operating *against* the functional activity of love. Such a dialogue "might have been named 'The Furies' " and it could have dealt with "the horrors lurking within imperfect realization." In *The Prelude* the shell, then, may be a part of the creative force somewhat like Whitehead's operative "Eros." But does Wordsworth think of anything comparable to Whitehead's sense of the furies as forces to be taken into consideration when we view the world? Is he merely optimistic?

In the *Prelude* account of the Arab and the symbolic shell there is an element comparable to that within such an imaginary dialogue as "The Furies," because Wordsworth does deal with tragedy. The shell, at the moment of the dream, sings a song of coming world-destruction, perhaps by a deluge. All this is connected with Wordsworth's report on his experience in reading. As the story unfolds, the Arab makes plans to preserve the two objects, the rock and the shell — the first of which "held acquaintance with the stars" and brought together man and man in a natural manner, though "undisturbed by place or t'me"; there is something in the human being beyond the material. Describing the symbolic shell Wordsworth, then, declares it

was a God, yea many Gods,
Had voices more than all the winds, and was
A joy, a consolation, and a hope. (107—)

The "winds" have voices. The reference to "winds" recalls to mind the effort in earlier thought to represent certain divine forces by comparable images. Angels are sometimes thought of as winds. But most important, in the passage quoted we may gather that for Wordsworth a literature that is lacking in a constructive or consoling power (when we are faced with a world in dissolution) is not a literature at its point of full greatness. What is needed ultimately is a "joy" or "hope," rather than any permanent dejection of spirits. This is implied in the "voices" flowing from the shell.

135

Wordsworth is including here a thought about pain and tragedy when presented in a form of beauty — or in art; these two forces, the painful and the tragic, are part of the scope of the literature or reading to which he makes symbolic reference. It is a literature of power. Everything exists for action, but, as Aquinas — building on Aristotle — suggests, there is an action which is based on something beyond any material entity. Such an action, or power, is what Wordsworth seems especially to have in mind when he speaks of the symbolic shell. The Psalms, associated with David, could be an example of this. Here we may think also of the joy that is often connected with the power-producing quality of the great Greek tragedies, as this joy — even exultation — is brought about through the artistic catharsis which Aristotle attempted to describe.

Earlier we have suggested that the human being and his works may be included in nature broadly conceived. Nature, indeed, embraces everything we know. Returning to a consideration of the passage in *The Prelude* about the stone and the shell, it may be observed, then, that one aspect of nature lies in the abstractions of pure mathematics to which man has given form; the other, represented by the shell, is to be seen in literature which may stand conveniently for man's artistic creation generally. These things are in the dreamer's mind as they are related to eternity symbolized by the sea. As the dream ends, the Quixote-like figure of the Arab disappears over the waste, with "the waters of the deep" (or eternity) in full pursuit.

To Wordsworth, the Arab represents the human being; he is a reality. He is therefore a figure deserving of reverence. There are enough men, the poet says, who in the event of some kind of flood would care for their "Wives, their Children, and their virgin Loves," but Wordsworth feels that he would especially "share the anxiety" of any person such as the Arab of the dream, and he would wish to undertake a "like errand." He would do whatever was possible to save the stone and the shell. Books and reading are important here. One could perhaps interpret the symbolism of the dream (and the statement that there would always be enough men who would try to take care of their families in the event of a cataclysmic disaster) as having a personal connection with the poet's life.

In Wordsworth's own case, this dream might have a bearing upon the fact that he left his daughter Caroline to the ministrations of her mother while he himself turned to his own pursuits — devoting his life for some ten or more years to his own concerns associated with building his career as a poet. He, like the Arab, was perhaps endeavoring to preserve the shell, and, if we include the other object, scientific and philosophic knowledge in general, he was also preserving the stone. Scientific and philosophic knowledge can of course be related to literature. All this — literature, science, personal experience, and philosophy — as a unit is part and parcel of power not only within the individual but within the race.

But the main purpose of the dream in *The Prelude* is of wider scope. One aspect of the tale is that the dreamer — clearly an outsider — had fancied himself seated alone in great distress of mind in what we would today refer to as a wasteland. He is filled with joy when he finds a fellow human being with him: the Arab, who also is an outsider. Seated on a dromedary, the Arab may well be able to make his way out of the waste, and there is, indeed, the refreshment of water available in the symbol of the dromedary, quite apart from the fact that the man might conceivably be able to make his way, in any event, to an oasis.

Then, ironically, there follows the *flood* of water; the very refreshment that they presumably need, and that may seem to be life-giving, turns into a potentially destructive death-dealing force. Before this happens, the dreamer, placing the shell to his ear, listens to a poem carrying a message of "passion" (the phrase in Wordsworth and many other writers has associations with the tragic), foretelling the physical destruction that is at hand. That destruction, we may say, represents in one sense

137

death — which is coming inevitably to the individual human being — but the individual can still devote himself to preserving the "elements" of science and song in so far as this may be possible before his passing.

The Arab had carried a lance "in rest," symbolic it seems of the possibility of such active enterprises as tilting against evils, though the symbol is also suggestive of the element of the Quixotic (tilting at windmills) which is to some extent intermingled in many idealistic efforts. Wordsworth's allusion to Cervantes seems suitable. Creativity such as that seen in *Don Quixote* contains, he holds, something of the divine. The whole story of the dream which he has reported affects the poet as a kind of entrancement. Such a feeling is comparable to that "deep entrancement" which he has felt when holding a volume of great literature in his hand — what he calls a kind of "earthly casket" which yet contains an element of immortality. This is what can be provided by "Shakespeare, or Milton" who are indeed "Labourers divine!" Some forty lines later he finds it necessary to recur with very special love to great literature

From Homer, the great Thunderer; from the voice
Which roars along the bed of Jewish song . . . (203—)

Wordsworth has been considering examples of literature which contributed to his growth as a person who is gradually attaining a clearer self-identity. There was the influence, also, of important works in English which, as he explains, are "more varied and elaborate"; along with these there were, in contrast, examples of the folk ballads of the common people. Such ballads he feels need to receive very special tribute. All of the popular poems, when excellent, are works "ever to be hallowed" in themselves, though they are less to be thought of as involving the hallowed, or the holy, than the human person himself, envisaged as part of the very being of destiny — deserving to be honored for his capacity of becoming, or of undergoing *process* pointing forever onward. The human being is, in a sense, a portion of great art, and the art is an ingredient of the person. Only nature as a part of a wider, more inclusive concept is to be revered more highly than supreme art. It is from nature that the great artist, observing and contemplating, derives what he needs for his art, nature itself in this sense being the veritable "breath of God." Here we have nature in its broadest sense.

At this point Wordsworth connects his reflections on books and literature with the problem of education, and the tendency of instructors to organize a young person's reading with a narrowly specific purpose in view. Organization with a certain degree of clear intention we can grant is necessary in education. However, it has potential dangers. It is best for the most part, Wordsworth feels — and he thinks Coleridge will be in agreement with him here — for a student to have an opportunity to range at will through the "pastures" of literature and not to be completely subject to a command performance on a prescribed diet of reading.

Thinking of the advantage of not being unduly "watched and noosed" brings to Wordsworth's mind the thought of his mother, who, though she died early, still was the "hinge" of all his "learnings" and "loves." Ann Wordsworth (like Wordsworth's foster-mother later) might be compared to a modern enlightened mother. She had self-integration. She was a woman without presumption or a clutching jealousy. It is evident in the context that she rejected — as Whitehead does — the idea that a human being is born evil. Such an idea is, to the poet also, a fanciful one, unless it could be accepted on an authoritarian basis. The whole problem of the rejection or acceptance of authority is an important one in Wordsworth and in other thinkers. At any rate, his mother had freed herself largely

From feverish dread of error or mishap

139

And evil, overweeningly so called ... (277—)

Wordsworth's mother, though she died early, had an important influence upon him. She was not, he says, a person who was "puff'd up" or "Selfish with unnecessary cares"; such fussy cares on the part of an adult, he believes, can be a burden to a young person. In these ways she exemplified unconsciously a standard of child development increasingly given respect in the psychology of today. Doubtless there are many errors which we have to face and correct in the matter of child rearing, but a point that the poet especially emphasizes is that his mother had merits not necessarily because her "faculties" were stronger than those that many other people have. Human beings with their inevitable limits are in general very much on a common plane.

Wordsworth recognized that it is an error to think that we can readily see through to the essence of the person, so far as the essential is connected with "faculties" or capabilities which are intrinsic. Standardized tests of abilities and intelligence had not been invented at that time, to be used for the purpose of stratification of people. The poet's mother had merits, possibly because of the period in which she lived — "from the times, perhaps," as he expresses it. The precise point at which we are influenced by a certain matter often makes all the difference in the quality of the person. But Wordsworth indicates the factor of space, which is also of importance in the end-result of what we are. It is an aspect of space-time that he is incipiently thinking of here. Considering his mother, then, he surmises that not only the time but "the spot in which she liv'd" may have been an influential factor in what she was. A realization that environment has a tremendous influence upon the nature of the individual is in the poet's mind.

Here as we think of Wordsworth's mother we may recall that "woman of a stirring life" and good sense who had somewhat similar traits — the peasant mother in the poem "Michael."

This shorter work was written in 1800 when the composition of *The Prelude* was in progress and, like the longer poem, makes use of a reflective, meditative style. The poems, as we have suggested earlier, can be thought of in relation to each other. In both works democracy is an underlying theme. The poet's thought does not tend toward the notion of class or of social superiority. But his present concern is books, stored knowledge and wisdom as related to life.

As Wordsworth in *The Prelude* still thinks of books and of the mind, particularly in youth, he re-emphasizes his feeling as to the mistake of trying, through a program of selected reading or other regimen, to force into development the mould of a "dwarf Man," or "worshipper of worldly seemliness"; such a child pedant is offensive to him. Crystallizing a young human being into a special form is destructive of values — and of whatever acquired "gifts" the child may seem to have. The kind of wrongly developed young person that the poet has in mind, as an example, is one who, though "shrewd," can yet "read lectures upon innocence," and who is completely in control of all his daily outward experiences. One weakness of such a child's development lies in the fact that, in the end-result, he has lost touch with common things and ordinary men. Yet such traits as this child has may pass in the world for genius:

Rank growth of propositions overruns
The Stripling's brain; the path in which he treads
Is chok'd with grammars . . . (323—)

This young person has "royalties" at his command which can be described as "telescopes, and crucibles, and maps." But what is the relation between Wordsworth's criticism of this youth and our consideration of philosophy? The answer is that fundamental thinking is required as a foundation for the education of every person, and in the example of the boy whom Wordsworth is holding up before us something that is very im-

141

portant has gone wrong. For if the individual has been undergoing this dubious process of growth the living being has reached a kind of death. The youth is hardly *alive*. His very soul is vanity, and once this, his center, has vanished,

> nothing is left which he can love.
> Nay, if a thought of purer birth should rise
> To carry him towards a better clime
> Some busy helper still is on the watch
> To drive him back and pound him like a Stray
> Within the pinfold of his own conceit . . . (357—)

Is there wisdom in Wordsworth here? We have to begin somewhere in educating the young person, and what could be better to use for this purpose than "telescopes and crucibles and maps"? Still, we have to reflect on our priorities. Wordsworth's criticism of conceit and vanity is, we see, emphatic. We often now say that belief in self is fundamental to a youth in attaining happiness in his home and in his school. This is correct. But may we not be frequently forgetting other selves in the school or in the home? Is the young person learning that the very nature of a self is that it is social? And if the sociality of concern is almost entirely lost may not the self become a misnomer? As Wordsworth reflects upon this problem broadly he conceives that the kind of youth he is considering may have been deprived of the value of fairy tales and other books of childhood. The poet feels deeply the danger of trying to bring up the young through complete anticipation of their every need. We may possibly see here the influence of Henry Fielding, whose novel *Tom Jones* — which was in Wordsworth's library — emphasizes a similar point. All along it is the importance of the use of books and stored learning which is the poet's theme, although it would be easy to lose sight of this fact in the present context.

But we can also relate Wordsworth's thought here to that of

Whitehead, referred to near the beginning of Chapter Four and again later, where emphasis was given to the importance of *imagination* in the process of learning. The point to be stressed and restressed is the role of the university or of any school in imparting ideas imaginatively. "At least," Whitehead says, "this is the function which it should perform. . . ." [3] In the total process, the effectual atmosphere of the school is for Whitehead of the utmost importance. "This atmosphere of excitement, arising from imaginative consideration, transforms knowledge." The context in Whitehead refers to university education, but the educational philosophy which is expressed is applied by him elsewhere to schooling at the lower levels.

The emphasis on the value of imaginative factors is prominent, then, in Whitehead's philosophy of education, and he relates it to the liberty of the self in an early chapter of *The Aims of Education*. As he says, "The only avenue towards wisdom is by freedom in the presence of knowledge." [4] In any education, formal or incidental to living, the environment about one is important in contributing to the process of change that takes place. In one's education, that very environment is always in a sense new, or being renewed. As he says three pages later, "The first procedure of the mind in a new environment is a somewhat discursive activity amid a welter of ideas and experience. It is a process of discovery. . . ." For this reason, *new* "environments" of various kinds should be subtly provided for discursive action in education.

The "discursive activity" which Whitehead speaks of here is the freedom to which we have referred. His subsequent comments emphasize not only what he calls the romantic aspect, which is under certain circumstances the general background, but also the importance of "wonder" and a wide use of freedom. There is a parallel to Whitehead's views in Wordsworth's consideration of education at the lower and higher levels. Both are concerned that through education one should attain spiritual power.

Wordsworth's famous "There Was a Boy" is connected with this idea of the need for freedom in youth. Speaking of this work Abercrombie says, "It can never, surely, lose its power by repetition," [5] and it has very frequently been given praise by others as a poem, in itself, considered in isolation. Wordsworth published it as a separate work, but it should be taken as an integral part of *The Prelude* where it also appears. The poet represents the case of a boy who was not confined like an "engine" to a road fashioned by others for the purpose of directing him mechanically. We are told that often, as the boy was surrounded by nature,

> the visible scene
> Would enter unawares into his mind
> With all its solemn imagery, its rocks,
> Its woods, and that uncertain Heaven, receiv'd
> Into the bosom of the steady Lake. (409—)

Aspects of the poetry here may be interpreted in more than one way. It is an *uncertain* heaven, symbolic in some degree of the transitory joy that surrounds the youth, rather than a certainty which "watchful men," feeling they are "skilful in the usury of time," would desire to attain — or in which "things," in other words, would control all "accidents." This point is emphasized further in the great turn in the passage, having wider metaphysical aspects, where we suddenly learn of the death of the youth of Winander who is being described. Everything, it is evident, cannot be controlled by rule and line. Here we see tragic irony, but an irony appears further in that, even as he writes, Wordsworth sees before his mind's-eye the green hill on which the village church sits —

> forgetful of this Boy
> Who slumbers at her feet; forgetful, too,
> Of all her silent neighborhood of graves ... (426—)

There is an effective ambiguity in these lines, projecting, as they do, the peacefulness, the serenity of the simple church on the one hand, and the seemingly all too easy acceptance of the fact of death, after a pitifully short time, by those who should presumably be closely concerned. But one may say that the event of death reduces in a great measure the conventional systems, and gives one pause. The conventional systems we refer to here are those tending to mechanize life such as that system followed by the all too-confident, more or less mechanical educator whom Wordsworth had earlier satirized.

The passage concerning the boy of Winander has a wider metaphysical character, but this feature will at present be discussed only briefly. The reader of *The Prelude* rather naturally dwells on the ideal aspects of the world that appear in relation to the boy and his experience up to the point of the sudden reference to death. Yet at this very stage the poet would have us think of the youth in his humbler aspect — in his actuality as a human being. Real youths must be recognized for what they are, with all their complex problems. They are

> not too wise,
> Too learned, or too good; but wanton, fresh,
> And bandied up and down by love and hate,
> Fierce, moody, patient, venturous, modest, shy;
> Mad at their sports like wither'd leaves in winds;
> Though doing wrong, and suffering, and full oft
> Bending beneath our life's mysterious weight
> Of pain and fear ... (436—)

The contradictoriness of childhood with its pains and joys and paradoxes — with mortality hanging heavily over it — very fittingly finds expression at this point in *The Prelude*. As Wordsworth thinks of books and education here one might expect him to give attention at once to the experience of *poetical* beauty. And the passage does contain such beauty. But actually he is immediately concerned with the problem of the attainment of knowledge. This is doubtless because in previous books of *The Prelude* he had been occupied with education and related matters very broadly considered. As a young person reads books or acquires knowledge it is important, in Wordsworth's view, for him to retain naturalness. There is also an over-all tone which is necessary to one's education: a tone which can give rise to depth of thinking. In Whitehead's view, likewise, if we were to emphasize educational discipline merely by itself, we would be thinking of a teacher's simple awareness that a student has been *sent* "to his telescope"; but in contrast to this mere sending of the student to the instrument there is another possibility of far greater wisdom, which would involve "the child's consciousness" that "he has been given free access to the glory of the heavens." [6] Here is the philosopher's "stage of romance" which is very important.

This statement in Whitehead about the heavens is by no means idle dreaming, and it has its application to power in education. For Wordsworth, too, education is more than the obedient accumulation of facts. What he is concerned about is not only learning, but wisdom. Power is here implied. We have previously noted (somewhat before the middle of Chapter Three) Wordsworth's reference to power and its presence "within our souls" in an especially private way in which "all stand single"; Whitehead, similarly, stresses power in relation to education. His remarks about a boy's school with which he was most familiar are pertinent. He is thinking of its relation to higher education. We do not stash away the contents of everything we have learned, he points out, and then later utilize any item according to need. "I can put my point otherwise by saying that the ideal of a University is not so much knowledge, as power. Its business is to convert the knowledge of a boy into the power of a man." [7] Wordsworth's earlier reference to power was related to feeling, as is the reference to Whitehead here.

What has all this to do with "Books" and "Stored Learning," the subject of our present chapter? Wordsworth feels that education comes through a combination of "doing" (external experience), reading, and spiritual growth. These ideas in *The Prelude* may be connected with certain profound, if rare trends in modern educational thinking. And it is at this point that the problem of power is before us once more. We can here recall Aristotle's persuasion that everything possesses existence in reference to its action — in its power to produce an effect. Book Five of *The Prelude* refers to the eye as having a very special "power"; and this energizing factor has a connection with education. What we have in mind here is knowledge that is united with an inward possession of power (the poet uses this word) by which such knowledge can be put to a more profound purpose than would ordinarily be possible. Nor is knowledge to be understood in the absence of the consideration of feeling. This as a doctrine appears in Whitehead also, in his discussion of the three forces connected in the rhythmic action of a viable education. But now we are to center our concern upon feeling, knowledge, and power as they appear in the poet.

These things can be illustrated to a certain extent in the account Wordsworth gives of a tragic experience which came to his attention on a twilight occasion when he walked on the shore of Esthwaite Lake where some "garments" had been piled, as the poet supposed, by a person who had gone bathing. Remaining in the area for some time Wordsworth became troubled. Darkness at last was falling. The effectiveness with which he brings out the quietness of the scene, as he waited, is enhanced by contrast through reference to "a fish up-leaping" and the accompanying slapping sound which broke for a moment the "stillness." But not only the quietness is reinforced. The vitality of the living, violently moving fish contrasts with the breathlessness of our ominous foreboding of death. There follows the account of the dredging of the water for the body of the drowned man.

147

The event of the drowning is not presented by Wordsworth as sensation merely in and for itself, however, but for the association it has with his reading and with the mystery of time and impermanence. It is also important in connection with his sense of the value of direct experience. As to experience, he distinguishes between terror and "vulgar fear." We may be cleansed or purged, it would seem, through terror, but "vulgar fear" is quite another, less helpful emotion. His "inner eye" had seen such things as he now observed in gruesome actuality, for he had read descriptions of comparable events even in the writers of fairy tales and romances. We can all remember fairy-tale horror exemplifying what he has in mind. His literary period was full of Gothic terror in fiction and drama.

But the conception he presents is that of tragedy undergoing a reconciliation within the mind as tragedy is reconciled in literature and in reflection. Such an experience as this tragic one which he had on the shore of Esthwaite Lake may well have connections in the mind, he says, which could provide a frame of reference assuming something of the "ideal grace" of "Grecian art." This sounds heartless, but it is not. The poet here is dealing with what we might call the roots of aesthetic experience — things that he believes are implanted in us in childhood.

In going on from the treatment of childhood to the consideration of youth and books Wordsworth tells us what a "precious treasure" he had in memory — for example, in certain of the contents he had noted in a small abstract of "Arabian Tales." This "treasure" will recall to one's mind the poet's view that a person actually is a memory to himself. Having found the small abstract, he later discovered that there were many other "Arabian" works of this kind which he could obtain from a vast "quarry" — more than once, in Wordsworth's writing, a book is likened to a firm foundational thing such as a rock. On hearing about this quarry of books he regarded the prospect of owning the large set of volumes as "scarcely earthly." He was so overwhelmed that he was prepared to cripple himself financially in order to obtain them. After months of scrupulous saving, however, he found that his resources were still too meager to make the splendid purchase a possibility.

In his "Father's House," nevertheless, he reveled in a "golden store" of works which he had not previously realized were there. Strenuously reading — indeed proceeding in a "devouring" spirit that was close to desperation — he came in the end to feel a sense of something almost evil in his preoccupation. Reading, that is, with all its merits, can be overdone. A philosophy of balance is required. To allay a feeling of guilt for having defrauded "the day's glory" through reading, he returned on one occasion to the outdoor sport of his ordinary activity with certain companions.

What, then, does all of this complicated autobiographical record in Book Five of *The Prelude* have to do with Wordsworth's work philosophically considered? What connection, furthermore, has it with actual poetry? As we think of the first part of this question, about philosophy, we notice that reflecting on the nature of books generally — or considering the place that they have in the life of a certain kind of person such as a poet — is itself a philosophical act. An examination of the place of books in our experience of fifteen-odd years of schooling, if generally considered, can be a significant part of the philosophy and self-understanding that we have attained. Wordsworth feels that he has only scratched the surface in regard to this kind of analysis.

If we consider the second part of the question, concerning actual poetry, we may ask somewhat more explicitly: What is the relation of the substance of this chapter to Wordsworth's poetry, or why, in presenting Book Five, is he writing a *poem* about this material? *The Prelude* analysis of the importance of books has a relation to his other works — such as "I Wandered Lonely as a Cloud," "She Dwelt among the Untrodden Ways," and "She Was a Phantom of Delight" — though the relationship is not immediately apparent. Reading is a central issue here, and it is a problem to which Elizabeth Drew and John Sweeney have given attention. For the general reader of a literary work it is the "power of amplifying and stimulating his sense of *living* which is its great human value." [8] This sense of the experience of living is what can be felt markedly in *The Prelude* and in Wordsworth's other poetry and it forms a part of Whitehead's philosophy in that he is concerned with "fully clothed feeling" [9]; such feeling, or ingression, is manifested in the short poems we have cited and especially in *The Prelude*. It involves going into or moving into the heart of anything.

There are other values in poetry besides the "great" one mentioned by the authors of *Directions in Modern Poetry*. But this prime value, the "sense of *living*," is close to the core of Wordsworth's emphasis in his work. In *The Prelude* he amplifies and stimulates a sense of living, though much of the "living" that he presents is connected with things that go on inside the consciousness. Inner and outer are almost equally balanced in his writing. Elizabeth Drew and her collaborator suggest that for the reader, "It is first and foremost the spirit of the poet that he hears and feels"; this indeed is true in the effect *The Prelude* has upon one.

We notice the spirit of Wordsworth even when he incorporates into his poem the discussion of Book Five which is given the unpromising title "Books." There is, furthermore, the decided emphasis upon the individuality of the poet implied in the statement about the spirit of poets which we have quoted from Drew and Sweeney, a point most highly applicable to Wordsworth. A poet, indeed, is a person who is intensely conscious of his own peculiar perceptions, concepts, and individual self-awareness. "One of the impulses behind" any poet's writing is not only that of interpreting experience for others: the purpose of a poet in regard to experience is "to clarify and objectify it to himself" [10]; and in Wordsworth, experience includes philosophy.

Here it will be helpful to consider a matter with regard to experience and its interpretation which is connected with Whitehead: the point being the difficulty in communicating which all people face. It is an idea concerning the theory that poetry deals with material which, if not quite incommunicable, is difficult at any rate to bring to clear communication. John Wheelock, whom we quoted near the middle of Chapter Three (on the "unsayable"), has brought out the matter exceedingly well. According to his theory the poet, prior to producing his composition, has tried to discover something, but has only half-discovered it. There is a problem here of the incomplete recovery of certain things that have been unconsciously disclosed. In the act of writing, an author learns what he has been in the personal process of recovering. Similarly, according to this view, "a child, when it begins to speak, learns what it is that it knows. And as a child will talk to itself, with no one around to hear, so in the poem the poet, it may be said, is talking to himself." [11]

But Wheelock makes haste to point out that the human race really "is one Self. Those 'others' are you." This process which he describes — including its application to both a writer and a reader — applies to all poetry. There is a connection between this view and that expressed in *The Prelude*. The point brought out in Wordsworth, and in Wheelock as well, emphasizes the extreme importance of process in our lives. By the conception of process we do not mean simply analysis. The world outside, or the non-self, to use Wheelock's term, is connected significantly with the world inside the self. This idea in effect appears in the closing pages of Book Five of *The Prelude*. "A gracious Spirit" is at work within man and without, and to some extent it has an effect on everyone, even those that "care not, know not, think not what they do"; continuing, Wordsworth suggests that there are values even in various types of the popular literature ordinarily regarded as beneath the consideration of serious readers. "Fiction for Ladies of their love,"

151

created by naive young male writers, are among the literary types of value that the poet has here in mind.

Similarly, according to Wordsworth, there are values in the literature of adventure. Even when the reader thinks he is idling away hours with such material it may at times have an important effect upon him. It may feed some useful "dumb yearnings" or "hidden appetites"; such literature, furthermore, has a close relation to that of one's reading in simple childhood. It does not, of course, usually provide the complete absorption or fully clothed feeling that Whitehead referred to in *Process and Reality*, since such ingression is not in its conception.

Wordsworth, as we have seen, repeatedly moves from the elementary to the lofty, and back again. Even in considering very light literature — in the fairy tales of childhood — he points out contrasting influences related to "earth" with influences related to the infinite. And, again, the problem of the adequate communicability of thought or feeling arises. A single word suggestive of process merely in the sense of analysis, or taking things apart, is an example. Thinking of things that are standard, such as standardized tests produced for commercialized purpose — where cash-return and business enterprise are important factors — will illustrate how feeling and thought may be compounded in different respects. The very conception of standardization would be repugnant to Wordsworth in a number of ways. Standards are needed. But there are questions we must raise. Whose standard, what standard, *why* this standard? In the last question there is the matter of what the particular standard will bring about or accomplish. Whitehead thinks of the problem of how a word may in one sentence represent something confusedly and in another context indicate something highly involved in a different fashion. Standards are important here. He cites the word "mortal" as an example of a term giving rise to complications. In his view the difficulty is not one of simple semantics, but goes deeper. "A precise language must await a completed metaphysical knowledge." [12]

All of the matters we have mentioned here have a connection with the philosophic problem of creativity, as Whitehead realized. Widely conceived standards and values are both important here. For Wordsworth, too, the creative or imaginative prospect which is offered to humanity includes

> Space like a Heaven fill'd up with Northern lights;
> Here, nowhere, there, and everywhere at once. (557—)

From the earlier stages in the childhood and youthful appreciation of literature Wordsworth proceeds to the problem of the enjoyment we have in a writer's manipulation of words and rhythms: things which one may value almost apart from the content. Reading can include memory or memorizing. He tells how in boyhood he memorized and recited poetry, doing it in a manner comparable to that in which he imagined birds carry on their singing. This was the outgrowth of the desire for something greater, "loftier," than the things which the average uninspired day itself would bring to one's reading. It is a form of activity paralleling the aspiring tendency that can appear within humanity. Related to this intimacy with literature at almost all levels, and intimacy with nature in "woods and fields," there is another nature to be found and valued in most important poetry. In the "motions of the winds" mysterious, perhaps divine presences are at work, and in these motions, which may be paralleled in the movement of words,

> darkness makes abode, and all the host
> Of shadowy things do work their changes there,
> As in a mansion like their proper home;
> Even forms and substances are circumfused
> By the transparent veil with light divine ... (622—)

Thus in *The Prelude*, as it was originally planned — that is, as a work to be completed in five books — Wordsworth present-

153

ed the growth of a poetical mind first through the early influence of nature, then through schooling and university experience (summed up to a certain extent in a consideration of his vacation after the first year at Cambridge), and on into somewhat more mature stages of life. Capping it all he presented a thoughtful analysis of the importance of books and literature to his inner growth. The discussion of books in *The Prelude* he regarded as all too scanty. His purpose was to consider his fitness — with his reading and general background — for the attempt to write a mature, major work "on man and nature and on human life." He grants at the end of his account that he has given an all too limited record of the significance of his reading, since he has confined himself to its relatively early stages. This admission he may have added to the conclusion of Book Five when he decided to resume his personal narrative in a sixth book, in order to expand *The Prelude* further. But that is a story yet to be unfolded.

For the present, however, the work was complete enough to be placed in Coleridge's hands as a kind of series of epistles which could be encouraging to him as an author and encouraging to Wordsworth also if it received Coleridge's approval as a treatment of the psychological and personal circumstances that produce poets and poetry. Coleridge took this five-book form of *The Prelude* with him on his travels to Malta and elsewhere, and finally lost it. Fortunately, Wordsworth had another copy of the work or we might not have been able to write this commentary, for whatever value it may contain. The next problem before us is to sum up a number of the important ideas which bring together Wordsworth and Whitehead and to point out the relationship between them to the extent that it has thus far been disclosed.

## Footnotes

1. *Process and Reality*, p. 516. See also pp. 517, 518, for sentences referred to in this paragraph.
2. *Adventures of Ideas*, pp. 188-189.
3. "Universities and Their Function," *The Aims of Education*, p. 139.
4. *Ibid.*, p. 47. See also p. 50, for quotation which follows.
5. Lascelles Abercrombie, *The Art of Wordsworth* (New York: Oxford Press, 1952), p. 122.
6. *The Aims of Education*, p. 51.
7. *Ibid.*, p. 43.
8. Elizabeth Drew and John Sweeney, *Directions in Modern Poetry* (New York: Norton, 1940), p. 22. The reference in the book quoted is to Blake but it actually applies to all poetry. See also p. 23.
9. *Process and Reality*, p. 82. This quoted phrase is especially fitting to Wordsworth, but see also Whitehead's praise of *The Prelude* in *Science and the Modern World*, p. 121.
10. *Directions in Modern Poetry*, p. 23.
11. Wheelock, "A True Poem Is a Way of Knowing," *What Is Poetry?* p. 27. There is a parallel here to Whitehead's emphasis upon process.
12. *Process and Reality*, p. 18. Note also Locke's words, quoted on p. 28 by Whitehead, " 'power' is 'a great part of our complex ideas of substance.' "

## Chapter VI

# *The Prelude*
# Expanded —
# Cambridge,
# the Alps,
# and Philosophy

Moving forward now into the material of Book Six of *The Prelude*, we may recall that to Wordsworth it appeared initially that, having told his life story down through the most influential aspects affecting his very young manhood, the essential substance for his purpose had been covered. Much of the formative side of his personality growth had been dealt with. But a presentation of the development of a philosophy, though it had been partly given, now presents a wider problem. Having completed his five books, he felt, it seems, that he could organize and clarify the continuing concerns of his life in a sixth book of *The Prelude* through proceeding to an account of some important things which had more lately happened to him. As we have explained earlier, he did not originally or at any time give the poem the title *The Prelude*, but nevertheless he thought of it all along as preliminary to writing that he wished to do later. We see in the gradual unfolding of *The Prelude* an illustration of the expansive literature to which we have several times referred.

Wordsworth had vast dreams concerning personality in rela-tion to his work, and he was aware also that the total con-sciousness of mankind itself — in its hopes and aspirations — had a great service to render to human beings. But the in-dividual personalities of his friends and of the imagined characters he portrays in very many works have a part in his life and his philosophy. His own personality, too, is a factor in this. That he should extend the account of the growth of a *poet's* mind, or of *his* mind, seemed altogether fitting in view of his interest in personality as such. Thus he could placate any qualms concerning egocentrism that he might have. There was also the fact that he was in any event developing his material for what value it could be to Coleridge's understanding of in-ner psychological problems. He and his friend, he knew, were very *personal* poets. But they were also literary men with a philosophical bent. Coleridge had reassured him as to this; the two authors were, indeed, a reassurance to each other. Presum-ably the philosophy that Wordsworth was evolving or strug-gling with in his present writing could be employed — or enlarged upon — in later more objective poetical works about people and the world. This was his ultimate aim.

Back in Cambridge as he is now in thought — if we turn to Book Six of *The Prelude* — he is "not so fond," he says, or im-mature, as he was when he left the university a few short months earlier for his summer vacation. Yet he is not so *eager*, he confesses, as he had been when he left his study in June. He is not, however, coming back quite like the youth Shakespeare refers to who returned to his study with "heavy looks"; indeed, Wordsworth says somewhat contradictorily, he was now "as gay and undepress'd" in his state of mind as when he had departed from the university. Books are still a lingering theme in his mind — just as we saw them to be in our previous chap-

157

ter. He turns to his reading willingly, though this means he is giving up other matters — among them the kind of pleasure he took in the companionship of the girls of "rocky Cumberland," with the "mirth" and "revelry" that association with them entailed. Seated in his "own unlovely cell" he now

> read more, reflected more,
> Felt more, and settled daily into habits
> More promising. (23—)

In the processes of his study many books were tasted and skimmed (here we may think of Emerson's way of doing much reading), but a large number of volumes were also devoured, or indeed perused, as he says, with studious concentration. It is significant that he reflects now, in the period after 1800, upon the processes of his reading when he was a university student. He would have given even more attention to an independent and studious plan of intellectual growth, he says, except that he was in a troubled state about his need for a practical career. He had some sense of guilt about a highly intellectualistic life, for he felt a responsibility to those who were back home and who doubtless, with some reason, expected exceedingly definite things from him leading to a recognized gainful profession. As a consequence he waivered, and indeed submitted as he says to a kind of tendency toward "cowardice" — ending up in far more indolence than befitted a person with his real sense of deeply underlying purpose. All these matters have a bearing upon the personality theme with which we opened the chapter.

The next two college years he chooses for the most part to skip, as he says, "without a separate notice." A reference in the poem makes clear that he is doing his actual writing about fifteen years after the events he describes — that is, he is writing in the year 1804. As he puts it, "Four years and thirty told this very week," he had been "a sojourner on earth," but the thrill of the "morning gladness" characterizing the first sense of being or becoming a poet had not passed from his "mind." Wordsworth refers, as he had done earlier, to the continued growth of his desire to be a poet, incidentally paralleling his personal evolution with a few words about a particular tree. The parallelism here involves the semiotic. This tree was an ash which he observed in the college yard, where he often remained by himself in the evening when the other students, anticipating the curfew, had left the grounds for the night in order to return to their rooms.

The tree, he says, had a "sinuous trunk" — suggestive perhaps of something within the poet Wordsworth himself. It was all overgrown with ivy in summer and especially "trimmed out," or made resplendent, with frost in the winter. In its loneliness and beauty it perhaps serves to some extent as a symbol of the nature of a poet, possibly with some suggestion of the frost-laden state of poetry in a given time or under certain circumstances — say, at a university. Wordsworth concedes that he may lack something of the magic found in the highest creative invention, but in the work of the earth there is a magic that cannot be gainsaid, especially in the spot where he had often stood

> Foot-bound, uplooking at this lovely Tree
> Beneath a frosty moon. The hemisphere
> Of magic fiction, verse of mine perhaps
> May never tread; but scarcely Spenser's self
> Could have more tranquil visions in his youth,
> More bright appearances could scarcely see
> Of human Forms with superhuman Powers,
> Than I beheld, standing on winter nights
> Alone, beneath this fairy work of earth. (101—)

The symbolic representation of the tree may well call to mind Whitehead's presentation of the symbolic in his volume *Symbolism, Its Meaning and Effect*. Wordsworth tells us that the fairy quality in the works of earth are for him, "bright appearances" of forms "with superhuman powers" which might be connected with mankind or attached to the general movement of humanity. There is, we would suggest, a still more complete symbolism in the passage in the picture of the tree with "exquisitely wreath'd" boughs. It is a symbolism which may be thought of in relation to the more elaborate symbolism referred to near the beginning of our discussion (in Chapter Five) concerning the stone and the shell, both treasured by the Arab or — since the incident really has application to the poet — valued by Wordsworth.

We can connect the poet's practice of symbolism here and elsewhere also with Whitehead's theory of the interpretive character of language — that is, of the interpretive usefulness of such an employment of expression. This is also true even in a mode of "usefulness," Wordsworth says, which is remote from the practices of the creative writer, and far less poetical. It is through the symbolic factor in much of our most ordinary perception, however, that error in thought may make its entrance, to our great disadvantage. But that very symbolic factor at many levels makes its contributions to our personal human insights. Indeed, those mistakes which may occur through our conscious or unconscious use of symbolic reference represent a price which, as Whitehead himself believes, the human race can gladly pay — for as he says, "Error is the mark of the higher organisms, and is the schoolmaster by whose agency there is upward evolution." [1] Whitehead relates symbolic reference here to "causal efficacy" involved in both "extensive interconnection" and in "potentiality." This sounds difficult. Some pages later he explains that "symbolic reference is the interpretive element in human experience." [2]

If symbolism has a place in everything that a human being does within experience, as Whitehead believes, its use is of the utmost importance not only to the artist of every kind but to each person, whatever his social level or activity. This idea is borne out from the point of view of psychology according to a statement by D.W. Harding that "the process of conveying a meaning beyond what is directly stated is one of the highly important features of ordinary language." [3] He stresses experience in its relation to aesthetics, but the subject he treats concerns generally not only symbol, emblem, and metaphor, but related forms of utterance. In the course of his discussion (two pages later) he distinguishes for convenience between two antithetical forms of expression: "The contrast," in a broad sense, is "between a representation that stands for something clearly definable and one that stands for something of which the general nature is evident but the precise range and boundaries are not readily specified, perhaps not usefully specified." The latter somewhat vague form of communication prominently involves the symbolic. Through it a poet produces some of his finest effects.

The ideas in Harding here and elsewhere parallel ideas in Wordsworth and hold an affiliation with those in Whitehead. They have a very profound application to poetry, and Harding himself says that this special "characteristic of symbolism is evident in some of the best of Wordsworth." [4] He takes issue one page later with a certain critic of the poet for holding that the "wealth of possible significance" in a given poetical passage is lost and that the poet "relapses into the mere description of scene." These are the words of the critic Tillyard as he makes his attack on the poet. Arguing against this, Harding points out that an object (a mountain peak) described by Wordsworth "by being embedded in a particular scene and event" does not lose its profundity; rather it "has a much more subtle and complex — and more uncertain — meaning than it could have had as a moral emblem drawn from nature." Harding's stress upon experience in its relation to symbolism parallels Whitehead's similar emphasis. It is furthermore characteristic of Wordsworth's writing. This is important. When Harding singles out Wordsworth's use of experience as

161

related to symbolism he is making a valuable contribution to the psychological interpretation of the poet. The whole problem of experience and symbolism in Wordsworth is so large a subject that an entire book could be devoted to it.

Previously in this chapter, in speaking of the tree overgrown with ivy in summer at Cambridge University, we mention that Wordsworth, in true humility, does not hide a sense of his own limitations. That is, he grants, for example, that he may lack something of the creative magic which characterizes fiction and poetic invention. He was "a better judge of thoughts than words" — as we might expect in an incipient philosophic poet. It was surely to his credit to keep his thought dominantly straight even though his words at this stage were often far from perfect. If the words chosen were at fault, the situation may be compared to the situation referred to by Whitehead when he speaks of "concentrating on a certain selection of sense-perceptions, such as words for example." [5] As he says, "There is a chain of derivations of symbol from symbol" and sometimes in such cases certain "relations, between the final symbol and the ultimate meaning, are entirely lost."

Now, as we consider the poet's case, he too had gone astray in his use of words, through not concentrating properly on the ultimate or final word and its meaning. The movement whether forward in the direction of a term to be chosen or backward toward the actual thing which is to be referred to can occur in either direction. Wordsworth, in his weakness, had gone astray partly, he says, through the common experience of youth; but more — he had been misled by his teachers and by his own habits of study. He was misled, that is,

by the trade in classic niceties,
Delusion to young Scholars incident . . . (127—)

Classical studies possess their excellence, Wordsworth says, but they are at a disadvantage not only in what we have just

162

mentioned but in the possible tendency of the student toward picking at phrases. Because of this fault the student may be forgetting the living flow of composition or overlooking the just characteristics of natural speech. This disadvantage in education is somewhat like that which Whitehead attacks when he describes a student working at his task of classical translation phrase by phrase, sometimes word by word. Such a dissection may be compared, he feels, to murder, and he quotes Wordsworth's own expression concerning those who "murder to dissect," though the poet used the expression in a somewhat different context from that in which the philosopher refers to classical studies.

Still, as we think of Wordsworth's present context — and his reference to classical "niceties" — it is almost as if Whitehead had read the passage shortly before writing his own observations on the classics in education during his day. If anything, the philosopher tends to be even more critical of humanism (in the sense of a central education in the ancient classics) than Wordsworth would be. Whitehead makes a plea for an early "sense of the unity of the whole" [6] classical work, or of any work, rather than a tendency toward picking at phrases. And he suggests a method whereby he believes better results could be attained. With Wordsworth too in *The Prelude* passage and elsewhere, there is a concern for the larger unity of things. This idea is exemplified when he speaks in summation of the weaknesses of scholars, the young and also the "old ones" who use

> that overpriz'd
> And dangerous craft of picking phrases out
> From languages that want the living voice
> To make of them a nature to the heart,
> To tell us what is passion, what is truth,
> What reason, what simplicity and sense. (129—)

It is evident here, and in the earlier reference in Wordsworth implying the pre-eminent place of thoughts in the act of composition, that the growth of broad intellectual power is basic in his conception of the evolution of a poet's spirit. Soon after making the statement from which we have quoted he comments on the relation of pure mathematics to the laws of nature. He is thinking here of the principles of science and the fact that they might well be made to be in certain respects "a leader to the human mind." The thought about science is significant because we think usually of poetry and the imagination when we reflect on Wordsworth's time in the romantic movement. But science was making very significant advances in the period. One need only think of the discoveries of Galvani in 1780 (when Wordsworth was ten years old), and those of Volta some twelve years later, to realize how important were the changing streams of scientific thought. The great work we have just cited actually "opened," according to Whitehead, "a new series of phenomena for investigation." [7] Wordsworth does well to speak of the importance of science as he does here in *The Prelude* and elsewhere.

Many other examples of this new scientific impulse might be given. Wordsworth could not, of course, be fully aware of how significant the relation of mathematics to the laws of nature would be in the century and a half to follow, but the direction of his thinking was definitely pointed toward the future. We have already seen evidence of his reverence for Newton. For the present we find him contrasting a surface view of the world of actualities with the abstractions of mathematics, and finding in the latter something more profound, more nearly absolute:

A pleasure calm and deeper, a still sense
Of permanent and universal sway . . . (151—)

Here Wordsworth felt that he was apprehending in the general character of mathematics a principle connected with the divine. Paralleling the poet to a certain extent, Whitehead speaks of mathematics and "the boundless wealth of deductions from the interplay of general theorems, their complication, their apparent remoteness from the ideas" in which the "argument" had its inception, "the variety of methods, and their purely abstract character which brings, as its gift, eternal truth." [8] We can wisely refer in this connection also to his essay "Mathematics and the Good" in which he touches upon Plato and "mathematical thought in relation to the search for the ideal." [9] So much at present for Whitehead. Wordsworth at any rate found in his own conception of the abstractions of mathematics that which is profound — indeed, a thing *approaching* the absolute. Here he was apprehending, he thought, a principle connected also with his conception of the divine, or with something which (as characterized by universality) was for him

> An image not unworthy of the One
> Surpassing Life, which out of space and time,
> Not touched by welterings of passion, is
> And hath the name of God. (154—)

Certain readers may question the value of a tendency to see in the study of the abstract (and in the study of mathematics) such significances as are suggested in this part of *The Prelude*. Wordsworth, they might say, had not advanced very far in his study of mathematics. But there is a depth in mathematics which may be perceived even in early stages of its study. Whitehead points out a situation in which one considers such simple things as "the relations of the number 'five' to the number 'three' " — that is, when one is "thinking of two groups of things, one with five members and the other with three members." [10] Here, he suggests, one is faced with a problem that is more complex than it appears to be on the surface. One is doing something remarkable when one is "entirely abstracting from any consideration of any particular entities, or even

165

of any particular sorts of entities, which go to make up the membership of either of the two groups." In his view such abstraction came about slowly: "It must have taken ages for the human race to rise to it."

Something of the wonder of mathematics and of its abstract character — even at the arithmetical level — may be perceived by a young student, and this wonder was recognized by Wordsworth. Aspects of it should be considered, Whitehead believes, by those who teach the relatively young. In a different passage he also observes that "the number 'two,' for example, is in some sense exempt from the flux of time and the necessity of position in space." [11] He follows this remark with a statement on the next page explaining how these "same considerations apply to the geometrical notions," and he points out, in connection with them, that Pythagoras, a forerunner in such ideas, "had hit upon a philosophical notion of considerable importance," one "which had a long history" connected with "theology." The history comes down in a significant way to the period of Hegel.

We need not now go into the further connection of such ideas with Whitehead's own philosophy; we will mention only that Hegel's life and contribution parallel in time the life and contribution of Wordsworth, both having been born in the year 1770. We shall have more to say of Hegel later. Thoughts related to mathematics such as those indicated in the last quotation from Wordsworth brought the poet, he tells us, a sense of peace which had a quality of the "transcendent"; the quality of peace had also for Whitehead a transcendence — a transcendence carrying one "beyond personality." [12] For Wordsworth the concept of peace possessed a quality of the poetical. This value he connects with the work of poets generally:

> So was it with me then, and so will be
> With Poets ever. (177—)

166

The particularities of the world may tend at times to dominate our life, but when we give our attention to them we may be struck by their impermanence. We have to consider, nevertheless, the lastingness of things. When we try to rivet attention upon it, according to Whitehead, we use images such as "the solid earth, the mountains, the stones, the Egyptian Pyramids, the spirit of man, God." [13] On the other hand, there is the fleeting character of life which is not sensed when we think of the great stones, mountains, and the various artifacts of Egypt. As the philosopher suggests, "integral experience" is often expressed effectively — though without encumbering detail — in aspiring popular religious feeling. And he adds the words, "One of the reasons of the thinness of so much modern metaphysics is the neglect of this expression of ultimate feeling." Such utterances of religious feeling (for example, in the song "Abide with Me") convey something which is also of importance to Wordsworth, and this is true, furthermore, of Whitehead. Utterances of this kind convey the feeling of permanency and also of transiency.

We have the problem, then, of figuring forth the fluid or, to use a word from Whitehead, the "fluent" aspect of objects. For Wordsworth, the particularities at times overwhelmed him to the point of domination — for example, in his tendency to value very greatly things in the world of nature and in his impulse to accumulate images from them. There was a danger, he says, that his other more profound and abstract impulse might be overpowered by his tendency to accumulate mere images. In poets, he feels, this concreteness is always a strong tendency which needs the counterbalancing of high abstract thought concerning

> an independent world
> Created out of pure Intelligence. (186—)

The effort to reconcile the claims of particularity and the

claims of the abstract presented to Wordsworth an important problem. And the same effort to conciliate the factors on both sides appears, though with greater subtlety, in Whitehead. Those things which "flow," or are perishing, decidedly have their claims in his philosophy. Without going into the intricacies of his solution of the problem of particularity and of the universal (indeed, he is troubled even by the very use of the two key words here), we may notice his statement in the page in *Process and Reality* from which we last quoted, that "Plato found his permanences in a static, spiritual heaven, and his flux in the entanglement of his forms amid the fluent imperfections of the physical world." Assuming that this is a fair interpretation of an aspect of Plato, we may observe that neither Whitehead nor Wordsworth is satisfied to reconcile the problem of the particular and the problem of the abstract, or the permanent, by minimizing the particular to that degree implied in this quotation concerning Plato. The philosopher thinks of the hymn "Abide with Me" in this connection.

Whitehead, indeed, finds a weakness in the subordination of the fluent world not only in Plato but in Aristotle and in Descartes. "This subordination," he says, "is found in the unanalysed longing of the hymn, in Plato's vision of heavenly perfection, in Aristotle's logical concepts, and in Descartes' mathematical mentality." [14] Newton, on the other hand, fortunately for the moment brought "fluency back into the world," though in somewhat too "regimented" a fashion. The degree of Whitehead's concern over "fluency" and permanence is evident in his remark that he devoted almost all of his long volume *Process and Reality* to the purpose of making an analysis of the "flow," or of the *perishing*, on a level which stresses, following Aristotle, an "analysis of becoming." [15]

That which perishes in our world presents, then, a great problem in Wordsworth and Whitehead. And we need hardly say that the question of the transiency of all things has contributed greatly to the melancholy moods approaching despair that one notices in various poets and philosophers, as well as in a variety of familiar forms of religious expression. In Whitehead there is a recognition of the place of melancholy in human thought, just as we find it also in Wordsworth. But in both Whitehead and Wordsworth there is, in addition, a large spirit of energy and joy along with the melancholy that is incidentally present. There is not a great measure of actual despair.

For the moment, however, we may consider melancholy in Book Six of *The Prelude*. Connected with Wordsworth's habits of abstracting, which he describes, there arose a tendency toward melancholy that may seem difficult to reconcile with what we have said elsewhere about his peace of mind. Perhaps we can explain it this way: since abstraction is for him related to eternal things, it can inevitably bring a sense of solemnity which could carry with it an attendant sadness. There was, however, a reason why this side of the poet's nature did not dominate him during his continued stay at Cambridge. It was partly due to a lack of intensity in his nature at that stage, he says, as well as to a kind of constitutional indolence which he possessed. From this point he goes on to the topic of friendship and of one's need for friends. He speaks to Coleridge here of his relations with his other very close intimate, Dorothy —

> she who hath been long
> Thy Treasure also, thy true friend and mine,
> Now, after separation desolate
> Restor'd to me ... (214—)

All three of these friends ultimately became extremely close in their association; all three had been bodily wanderers and were, even when together, wanderers of the spirit. They were searchers. The need of friendship is a very important subject in *The Prelude*. Indeed, the whole poem is largely based upon it. All this has a connection with the theme of personality which we mentioned near the beginning of the chapter. The poet's thoughts about melancholy, as well as about peace, a "transcendent" peace, bring him, however, most particularly to reflection about Coleridge and the needs of Coleridge's nature. Wordsworth's basic purpose in his present writing is to give comfort to Coleridge

wandered now in search of health,
And milder breezes, melancholy lot! (249—)

It is a melancholy lot that Coleridge faces not only because of his lack of good health, but because he is without his friends. As we have mentioned somewhat earlier in this chapter, Wordsworth refers both to the moment of his writing, in 1804, and to a time some fifteen years in the past when he was at Cambridge. Now in thinking of his own days at the university and of Coleridge's present travel to Malta, he also reflects on Coleridge's boyhood at Christ's Hospital in London. There the boy Coleridge pursued "subtle speculation" — "abstruse" labors over the medieval thought of the "Schoolmen," as well as ponderings over "platonic forms," which, as Wordsworth describes them, are represented by "wild ideal pageantry"; at this stage of *The Prelude* we have the author's handling of time and we return to the theme of abstraction which, we are told in the poem, involves bringing together things that are disparate one from another.

The general emphasis upon abstraction mentioned earlier may well be recalled in this connection. For Wordsworth it was considered of special importance in the educational ideals that deserve to be followed, and for Whitehead it held a similar place as can be seen in *The Aims of Education*. Again, we find in one of Whitehead's other volumes, *Modes of Thought*, a similar stress, though of broader implication: "The growth of consciousness" is itself "the uprise of abstractions." [16] Wordsworth, as we saw, realizes the extremely stimulating value in Coleridge's interest in the abstractions of Plato and other

170

thinkers, but senses both the advantages and disadvantages that may occur if the relationships considered are based on matters "well match'd or ill," for there is always the danger of using mere "words" instead of keeping our eyes sufficiently upon actual things. Whitehead also stresses both points: the concentration involved in abstraction, he says, leads on the one hand to unification and increased mental energy; however, "this enhancement of energy presupposes that the abstraction is preserved with its adequate relevance to the concrete sense of value-attainment from which it is derived." [17] In reading the related passages in Book Six of *The Prelude*, one feels these remarks by Whitehead might almost have been uttered by the poet himself.

Wordsworth's main purpose now is to move as rapidly as possible toward his experiences in London and abroad. This is the subject of the crucial latter part of his young manhood which he had not originally planned to include in the five-book *Prelude* as first conceived. He says again that he also, like Coleridge, knew what it was to be a wanderer in many ways, and such references lead to an account of his walking tour across France and Switzerland after he had completed his third year at the university. This trip was a subject he had earlier dealt with — in his volume *Descriptive Sketches*, of 1793 — but he felt that he could now give the material a different and better emphasis. He was attracted to France and Switzerland not because of the possibility the trip offered of an accumulated knowledge of the world or because of the opportunity it presented to observe human beings and the events of his time, but mainly, he says, because of the anticipated delight in the scenery of the Alps. This was the state of his mind as a young student moving toward the stage of the completion of his college years.

The poet's hopes in regard to the scenery were indeed expansive or sanguine. "Nature then," he says, "was sovereig'n" in his "heart," for "mighty forms" (perhaps the Alps) had seized upon his "youthful Fancy"; thus he had received "a charter to irregular hopes." Why are the hopes irregular? The passage would seem to suggest that in Wordsworth's writing of 1804 he did not have a naive idea with regard to a sentimental nature worship. The account of the journey includes reference to the development of the individual under the influence of nature in stages such as we may see mentioned six years earlier, in his "Tintern Abbey" poem. But there is one exception which has been often noted. The difference that can be seen in *The Prelude* is that greater emphasis is paid to the development of an active mental principle which is aided by the use of the highest imagination. Wordsworth speaks of melancholy in its casual character, and he then turns to a far different dejection, "a deep and genuine sadness," that came to him in his travels.

This occurred after he had climbed upward on a certain track in the Alps, only to learn from some peasants who were passing that he should have made a different turn and proceeded downwards. For he had already passed the highest point of the divide: he *"had crossed the Alps."* The italics are in *The Prelude.* Is the material fact of reaching the highest spot in a peak or a ridge important? Why at this point was he melancholy? Wordsworth on these travels had a companion with him: Robert Jones; but the poet's private thoughts are our present concern. He had probably looked forward to the moment of being at the final ridge of his ascent, but all feeling of any such supreme moment was lost in the confusion of the surrounding cliffs and mountains. Great ranges and peaks of the world are not clearly and easily analyzable by means of the immediate glimpses one has when one is so close. All perspective is lost. They are not in the least like the obviously discernible mountains of the English Lake Region. Wordsworth and his friend, at any rate, having for the present mistaken their road, lost also a moment of climax which they were anticipating. In a sense it seems that to the poet from now on, in descending, he was traveling merely along with the current of a stream. The figure with regard to the flowing river which they were following may be taken symbolically.

The rest of their whole journey was to be, in general, downwards. The greatest thrill of being in the Alps was not what he had supposed. As this was borne in upon Wordsworth, somewhat confusedly, he was struck by his situation and he had a momentary feeling of dullness. Then imagination took over and he "was lost as in a cloud"; he had been stopped without even "a struggle to break through." Now, however, at the time of writing this portion of *The Prelude* some fourteen years after the event, he no longer feels the sense of dismay he had experienced in Switzerland. At such a time, in a kind of climactic moment, he tells us, if the imagination may begin functioning effectively, all

> light of sense
> Goes out in flashes that have shewn to us
> The invisible world . . . (534—)

Through imagination greatness may make its "abode" when the circumstances are ripe. Wordsworth does not say that imagination is alone necessary for this result. He relates the idea concerning imagination to the concepts of infinitude, hope, and effort. The central idea here is one of aspiration and the sense of something that may be constructed not altogether mechanically. It is beneath highly activated "banners" that the mind operates, thinking not of "spoils or trophies" nor of anything attesting "its prowess"; the mind, that is, in the end has its blessing through conceptions having "their own perfection and reward" and is thus

> Strong in itself, and in the excess of joy
> Which hides it like the overflowing Nile. (543—)

Wordsworth, having learned that he had actually crossed the

divide, suffered, as he emphasizes, a certain feeling of "slack-ening" when he continued on his way beside the enlarging stream. Proceeding downward some moments later there came to him in the midst of a noisy gorge a renewed joy, including feelings of "tumult and peace"; these feelings, he says, comprised a sense of the workings of the universal mind which may lead one to some partial understanding of "the types of eternity." This is an important moment in *The Prelude*. The author touches very briefly upon revolutionary events which were occurring in the country round about him during his walking tour, but in his journey on that particular summer these occurrences seemed only incidental compared to his opportunity of viewing the scenery of the Alps.

That night Wordsworth stayed at an inn that he referred to as a hospital. This was at a point where two streams met in "confluence." All night long he felt deafened by the noise of waters. In the morning, continuing on his way, he reached Lake Como, that "treasure of the earth," and thereafter proceeded "from town to town" by linked "pathways roof'd with vines," passing onward almost like a "sunbeam" or like a breath of air. Here the intangible imagery may reveal to us that it is to the mind, not to external things, that he would give tribute. The mind, that is, values, treasures up, or utilizes to greater purposes such experiences as the poet enjoyed.

And there is perhaps something of Whitehead's "symbolic reference," which has been mentioned earlier, even in the imagery which the poet uses describing how he traversed the region, and "pass'd" in movement "without pause"; again we have an emphasis upon the problem of stable permanency beyond all "motion" and the sense of "passage" (in Whitehead's term) that is a continual thing. The question of the objective and the subjective — as it may be put for the present — is given emphasis when near the end of Book Six the poet tells us that the mind must not be regarded as if it were a "mean pensioner" dependent upon "outward forms"; it is more. But he never states this case in such a way as to negate altogether the claims of passivity on the one side or activity on the other. Rather, his philosophy would seem to emphasize, as does Whitehead's, the importance of organism, not that of a static or crystallized reality. Such a broad tendency towards organism gives rise in itself to an expansiveness in literature.

Wordsworth does not accept a frozen view of things — or, to use Whitehead's expression, "the one perfection of order" [18]; this kind of false perfection the philosopher criticizes by implication again and again, and incidentally he attributes it, somewhat regretfully, to certain of Plato's dialogues. For Whitehead the universe must be conceived in terms of anything but a static view: it must be thought of as "more various, more Hegelian." The tendency of Wordsworth's thinking, likewise, does not call for any single perfection of grand structure. His view represents anything but a stasis. We may recall that Wordsworth, as we have mentioned, stressed an activity-principle comparable to that in Hegel. And we may stress again the fact (mentioned near the middle of this chapter) that he, like Hegel, was born in 1770. Something of the Hegelian variousness of the world, as it presented itself to the poet, may be seen in his representation of his experiences later which will be given subsequent treatment in another volume.

### Footnotes

1. "Symbolic Reference," *Process and Reality*, p. 256.
2. *Ibid.*, p. 263.
3. D.W. Harding, *Experience into Words* (New York: Horizon Press, 1964), p. 72. See p. 74 for the next quoted material in our text.

4.  *Ibid.*, p. 79; see also p. 80 and p. 81 where Tillyard is criticized. For Harding a proverb also has a relation to the symbol; see Harding, p. 72. Wordsworth as a poet takes a special interest in epigrammatic forms of expression because of their concentratedness.

5.  *Symbolism: Its Meaning and Effect*, p. 83.

6.  *The Aims of Education*, p. 110.

7.  *Introduction to Mathematics*, a Galaxy book, revised edition of 1948 (New York: Oxford, 1958), p. 20.

8.  *The Aims of Education*, p. 118. Whitehead's view of the matter undergoes change in later works; nevertheless, he let this passage of 1917 stand in 1929, with the feeling that readers would give careful attention to his later views. He *was* close to Wordsworth in 1917 in the respects we have indicated.

9.  *Essays in Science and Philosophy*, p. 75.

10. *Science and the Modern World*, p. 30. See our Chapter II, footnote 5.

11. *Ibid.*, p. 41.

12. *Adventures of Ideas*, p. 371. See also p. 375 and the reference to the "conformation of purpose to ideal beyond personal limitations. . . ." See also the reference to transcendence on p. 380.

13. *Process and Reality*, p. 318.

14. *Process and Reality*, p. 319. Whitehead is referring to the hymn "Abide with Me."

15. "Process and Reality," a short commentary in *Essays in Science and Philosophy*, p. 89.

16. *Modes of Thought*, p. 168.

17. *Ibid.*, p. 169.

18. *Essays in Science and Philosophy*, p. 90.

# What Has
# Gone Before —
# Seen in
# Retrospect

Both Wordsworth and Whitehead have a broad view of life
with a strong psychological and philosophical emphasis. The
sense of the psychological in their writing accords significantly
with certain modern developments occurring from their time to
our own period. The two thinkers, one primarily a poet and the
other a philosopher with poetical perception, have, furthermore, a sense of the importance of an activity-principle within
the self, and they strongly believe that this feature in human
life has significance in relation to a philosophical insight. In
Chapter One, on "Childhood and School-Time," we have seen
that, along with activity, both an inner emphasis and an outer
application are stressed in the works of the two figures. Such
an emphasis is fundamental for them in a life-view in which
an insight into emergence plays a part. In their work
emergence has a relation to aspiration. A strong social

emphasis, including a democratic philosophy of equality, also appears in their writings. In this connection they have a firm belief in a spiritual and an actualistic sense of community.

Whitehead refers critically to a "sensationalist mythology." [1] In doing so he attacks the tendency toward an exclusively mechanistic approach to life. Here he parallels Wordsworth. But both men in an actualistic way emphasize and re-emphasize the point that further realistic advance in a social and truly human liberty is essential, and they especially stress the conception of value. Whitehead in his writing shows an appreciation of the breadth of Wordsworth's outlook on life. He quotes, as we saw, from a prose preface to the poet's *Excursion* which tells about the value of a philosophical poetry "containing views of Man, Nature, and Society." [2] What he sees in this concerning the social accords with a part of his own thinking.

The triple goal referred to by Wordsworth in *The Excursion* preface (including the importance of individual man, nature, and society, or the social) represents certain vitally important tendencies in the poet's thought, but includes essential features of Whitehead's own philosophy as well. It is for this reason largely that he quotes the passage from Wordsworth. Exceedingly significant, in an even more penetrating way, is the philosopher's reference to Wordsworth's prehensiveness, the concern for profound and "full concrete experience." These are Whitehead's own words about what he finds importantly in Wordsworth's writing. He sees in the poet a vivid and actual ideal represented in Wordsworth's very perception.

Considering the material we presented in Chapter Two, on "*The Prelude* and Later School Days," we may observe the aspect of the poet's thought in which, while rejecting any belief in materialism, he nevertheless does not fall into a morass of subjectivism, a danger concerning which the philosopher is also sensitive. We cannot here recapitulate many of the features previously covered about this, but it is education itself, in its implications, which is the main continuing theme

178

throughout the second chapter. The discussion is not at all on the external classroom experience, which one might expect to see emphasized. Inner self-unification and social unification receive prominent stress. In Whitehead, too, we see the recognition of a danger in any undue emphasis on merely external relationships, educationally or otherwise. The two men are in this respect markedly together.

Features that we have just mentioned concerning self-unification and the dangers of merely external relationships may be helpfully considered through glancing at the reflection of Thomas Hill Green, a philosopher representing a generation preceding that of Whitehead. Green forms a kind of bridge between Wordsworth and Whitehead, especially in what amounts to the attack on mechanism and materialism, and he undoubtedly influenced the young Whitehead, although Green died when Whitehead was twenty-one. Green, like Whitehead, was an admirer of the work of Wordsworth. He saw in it something of the quality of philosophic "revelation" (we quote Green's word), although he stresses also the importance of another factor found in the poet: that of a dynamics which would aim to work "actively" (this again is Green's term) in relation to life; the very special emphasis Green would make, however, while he is thinking about Wordsworth, is upon the poet's sense of inner peace whereby the human mentality may "attain to that harmony with itself and the divine idea which is the key of all knowledge." [3]

Though Green died in 1882, his voice represented something like an illumination for many thinkers in a period down to the beginning of the twentieth century and even later. He stresses the importance of the merging of classes, one into another, and the idea of community, strongly emphasized later in George Herbert Mead. What Green seeks is "one social organism." [4] Green's wide use of the conception of organism, here and elsewhere, recalls the thought of Wordsworth and does so in an emphatic sense comparable to that in Whitehead.

179

Mention of Green is made at this point because of the light his philosophy throws upon the concern of Wordsworth and Whitehead about other problems that are very much with us to-day. Green is highly conscious "of positive social injustice, of oppressive social custom, or simply of deficient sympathy." It is easy to be blind to these factors when we live, as Green says, in circumstances comparable to those of the restricting cave to which Plato refers. Green gives special emphasis to the cave, almost with psychological perception. Like Wordsworth and Whitehead Green speaks of the dangers of dogma and the limitation of the mind which dogma often causes. He pursues problems in the modest spirit of making an inquiry; like the poet and Whitehead, he would always preserve the individual's right to independent thought. Green furthermore may be link-ed with Wordsworth and Whitehead in regard to matters con-cerning education. Because of space limitations, this feature, although it could be illuminating, will not be developed here.

Our Chapter Three, in its treatment of Wordsworth's "Cam-bridge University Days," brought out the fact that Wordsworth and Whitehead are both down-to-earth in their insights into life, although this merit in their thinking may easily be missed by a casual reader of their work. Both men held, furthermore, what might be called a common faith — that is, a constructive faith within the reach of a common creative humanity. All human beings are for them capable of being creative. In Words-worth and Whitehead, also, there was stress on the importance of a vivid and lively imagination. Everyone needs to develop this faculty. But the poet and Whitehead provide corrective factors to an overweening fancifulness. In both men the impor-tance of universal good sense is a striking feature, as indeed is the need for a corrective to the tendency toward an unduly stressed or presumptuous self-estimate. There are many subtleties in the thought of both Wordsworth and Whitehead: for example, in the poet's references to immortality and the philosopher's similar concerns. These subtleties we shall not

180

summarize here, for a concise statement about this would involve too great a loss of what had been developed in the substance of our earlier, more complete discussion.

The observations we have heretofore presented gain further value through reference to our Chapter Four, concerning Wordsworth's "Summer Vacation after the First Cambridge Year"; in that section we saw the poet returning to the problem of self-growth, a subject that we can also observe notably in Whitehead. Wordsworth at a certain point becomes, he says, "self-transmuted," and similarly there are profound changes that occur in Whitehead during his personal self-development. The volumes he has written represent eloquently, even profoundly, his self-growth through his reading and through his reflection as a philosopher. But though both men have an important concern for the self, they contemplate, too, and they emphasize, the difficulty of the great problem of the essential rights of human beings and the spiritual importance of others. They have a sense of the fact, emphasized in our modern thought, that those others are you. In both there is a marked tendency directed toward leveling, as well as toward aspiration.

Here, as we think of aspiration, we may recall Thomas Hill Green once more because of his steady and prolonged interest in the significance of the aspiring self. Both Wordsworth and Whitehead may be brought into relation with Green in regard to aspiring as connected with the problem of immortality. The tendency to deny the possibility of immortality in a sense is for Green a maintenance of the "destructibility of thought, and this is a contradiction in terms, for destruction has no meaning except in relation to thought." [5] Here the word *to* might have been underlined. The conceptions of all three men on this great question would deserve wider study than we can here give it. Our discussion of the books of Wordsworth's *Prelude* included in its latter portion a continuation of the poet's preoccupation with inner and outer education, and there is a relationship, we can stress again, between this concern and the philosophy of Whitehead. For Whitehead there is the long, complex process of growth and emergence, including the potency of education in general human development as well as in the gradual development of the individual as a self.

In Book Five of *The Prelude* we find Wordsworth absorbed in the place that reading has in the growth of the power of the individual self. The idea of self-power appears also in Whitehead, as it has its very significant place here in Wordsworth. These are factors which we follow in our Chapter Five. Power is obtained through moving into the heart of things, not through being exclusively centered upon externals. According to the poet "A gracious Spirit" is at work within the self, and something of this view may be found in the philosopher, especially as it may be brought operatively into function within human beings everywhere, if they strive toward largeness, or are enabled environmentally to work towards a large purpose. This is part of Whitehead's philosophy. Striving and opportunity are both necessary. The "gracious Spirit" for Wordsworth is a force at work in the universe outside ourselves, but is also functional within the person. The inner self needs to be in profound interrelation with that which is outside. In the philosophies of Wordsworth and Whitehead there is a distinct religious element, which is exemplified here.

Whitehead has similar views to those of Wordsworth in that it is not a mere religiosity or a cold analytical religion that claims his allegiance. In the poet and in the philosopher, religion leads to action and to what may be accomplished for human development most broadly considered. Religion, that is, forms a definite part of their philosophy. It is not the favored few or the elect that we should have in mind when we consider this. For Wordsworth, as he thinks of books and the creativity of literature, there is a vast space open for human beings — a space wide as the heavens. In the case of the philosopher likewise there is stressed the importance of symbolic creativity

182

as well as a spirit of spontaneity in the bearing that creativity has upon an individual and upon social living. Creativity can be marked by transfiguration.

A full sense of what Wordsworth in his first intention was working toward cannot be gained from a consideration of the five-book form of *The Prelude* as he had at first planned it. In our Chapter Six we refer to the new material that Wordsworth chose to include in continuing his poem. This new substance contains a symbolic reference to a tree at Cambridge University. The inward and outward character of life concerns him. We see nature in the abstract represented in the tree, and we prehend, we could say, the presence of nature in the surrounding world of the seasons, as well as in the active internal world of the one who perceives the tree. Symbolism, too, has a vital place in the philosophy of Whitehead. We can well imagine him, under the influence of Wordsworth, looking also at a symbolic tree at Cambridge in his college days. Not only symbolism should here be stressed but the thought that produced it. Symbolism is at work for him everywhere. But to return to the poet. Wordsworth, at the point we had reached, refers to mathematics, and symbolism has a connection here. Thereafter he proceeds to a number of comments upon an approach to infinity and the divine.

Following the presentation of these thoughts he describes his youthful experience in traveling through France and into the region of the Alps. The experience enables him to touch upon the conception of the immense as well as on that of eternity. He had not been able, he says, to *observe* the highest point in crossing the mountainous divide, but in going down toward Italy in a spirit almost of flowing, all feeling of "sense," or of sensation passed, at moments, away from him, and he had a self-vision that reached toward an "invisible world"; circumstances were at that time ripe for him to appreciate what he regarded as a sense of higher reality, and this feeling brought a vision approaching that of infinitude. It also brought a sense of vital hope. It is not his own individual "prowess" that aids him and that he thinks of here. But it is nevertheless an abundant joy that he feels — actually a super-abundant joy. There are echoes of Kantian antinomies, or contradictions, that are present in such an experience. For example, there are contrasting feelings including "tumults" as well as "peace" (the poet's words), but these feelings bring him "types" of what he thinks of as the eternal.

Thus it was that he passed down from the Alps, proceeding not as a "mean pensioner" dependent exclusively upon that which is "outward," or upon the sensory, but as a human "soul" (his word) that has, in the utmost reaches of being, something closely affiliated with a surrounding world. That surrounding world as in Whitehead is a gigantic world of organism. This live and creative world receives expansive and inspiring treatment not only in Wordsworth but in the philosophic realism elaborated in Whitehead, which, though it is realistic, has affiliations, nevertheless, with an idealistic outlook toward the universe.

That basically realistic view which the philosopher developed is characterized by unity and complexity. It is a view which comprises the variousness of the world, as we said at the end of the Chapter VI, where we referred to Hegel, but it goes beyond him in that we have no absence of the concern for persons as individual beings, and it leads to a greater multifariousness in its large unity than that to be found in Hegel. It is concerned with the person, as Martin Buber is concerned with the very personal you — with the thou. Here we are thinking of the *thou* as you, and as countless other examples of the thou in the entire world. But we are thinking also of a Thou that is larger: one that includes the universal and the universe, and all that is existential within it. There is also the problem of space and time which needs to be unfolded more fully in another volume that we plan to complete.

But to return to all that which is an existence within the

universe of the impersonal and the personal; in the interpersonal outlook we are in need of you and of others who, together, are ourselves. The germ of this idea may be seen in the words of Adam Smith when in 1759 he speaks of the power of "the spectator to enter into the sentiments of the person principally concerned" and the fact that "the person principally concerned" can "bring down his emotions to what the spectator can go along with"; here Adam Smith sees in close relationship "two different sets of virtues." [6] Stressing his thought at an emphatic point at the beginning of a chapter, he is thinking both of the tendency toward "humanity," on the one hand, and "self-denial" on the other hand. On the next page he refers to the importance of the "gesture," and its relation to "equitable sentiment" and he is thinking of the other as our neighbor. Adam Smith's reflections, then, are not limited alone to those concerning the economic man.

George Herbert Mead gives very strong stress to gesture and the sharing which economic relations can give rise to. We think of large economic markets — and their extensiveness is important; these markets in the end lead to "a more highly organized society"; the fact of the market makes something new out of "groups" which had been *isolated* from each other so that later the new situation produces "partially unified groups." [7] In the long run economics tends to give rise to something more than individual personal wars. Mead implies that we should avoid acceptance of the limitation involved in the theory of the basic ruthlessness in trade relations. The abrasiveness of this theory is signalized in the simplistic formula *let the buyer beware*. There is more than this in economics. Business, in its development and contribution to mankind through the years, represents importantly an interaction — something greater than an over-simplification involving merely conflict. But even though co-operation has been important in economics, conflict, of course, has also existed.

Near the close of our Introduction we spoke of Mead's socially oriented philosophy, his emphasis upon community, and we also referred to the breadth shown in the more recent books of John K. Galbraith, where the perspectives can be likened in many ways to those shown in the breadth of Whitehead's interactive philosophy. A book could well be written on the relation of Whitehead's world-view to that of Galbraith. The sense of community was likewise important to Wordsworth; indeed, he refers specifically to the "spiritual community" binding us "the living" together with all ages of the past. [8] And he immediately follows the sentence in which he brings out this point with another reference to "community" and its importance. For Wordsworth, as for Whitehead, the wealth of nations, internationally considered, cannot be thought of as the wealth or money of "economic man" only, but it includes a certain richness of life that greatly needs to be sought.

*Footnotes*

1. *Process and Reality*, p. 214.
2. *Science and the Modern World*, p. 118. The quoted expression is from Wordsworth, as given by Whitehead.
3. *The Works of Thomas Hill Green*, ed. R. L. Nettleship, sixth Impression (London: Longmans, Green, 1911), III, p. 15. Green is discussing the influence of civilization on genius.
4. *Ibid.*, p. 41. Green's topic here is "An Estimate of the Value and Influence of Works of Fiction."
5. *Ibid.*, p. 159. There is an important difference between Green and Whitehead that we cannot consider here; that difference concerns Green's tendency toward the absolute.

6. *The Theory of Moral Sentiments*, with an introduction by E.G. West (New Rochelle: Arlington House, 1969), p. 26.
7. *Movements of Thought in the Nineteenth Century*, p. 171.
8. Notes to *The Prelude* (Text of 1805), p. 312.

# Index

*This short index excludes certain names*
*frequently referred to in the book*